JAMES

A SELF-STUDY GUIDE

Irving L. Jensen

MOODY PRESS

CHICAGO

Contents

Introduction

The Bible dwells mainly on two themes: "The Way to God" and "A Walk with God." No one can walk *with* God who has not first been restored *to* God. Much of the New Testament tells us the way a sinner can come to God and be eternally saved. That way is by God's grace, through one's faith in Jesus Christ (Eph. 2:8). The epistle of James, on the other hand, was written to instruct Christians—those who have been reconciled to God through Christ—how to walk with God in this present life.

Thoughts, words, and deeds are the ingredients of a person's daily living. The important question here is, What *kind* of thoughts, words, and deeds should be part of the life of a Christian who walks with God? James was written to give us God's answers to that question. It will be of great benefit to you as you study this epistle to remind yourself continually that these answers originated with God, whose Word is infallible and intended for your eternal welfare. Pray that God will make you the kind of Christian He appeals for in this epistle.

Suggestions for Study:

Basic Bible study in one's mother tongue can and should be direct, personal, inspiring, unencumbered with technicalities, practical, and enjoyable. The study suggestions given below follow procedures that are consistently applied in the manuals of this self-study series.

1. Spend most of your time with the Bible text itself. Don't read into the text any meaning that is not there.

2. Let context—the surrounding words and phrases—be your ally in interpreting any particular passage.

3. Train your eyes—physical and spiritual—to keep seeing things in the text. Don't be content with a casual, quick glance.

Comprehensive analysis is mandatory for maximum learning. This can be the most enjoyable part of your study.

4. Compare modern versions with the King James Version reading for help in determining the full meaning of a word of phrase. But do all your analysis in the basic study text (the King James Version is the text used in this manual).

5. Be continually on the lookout for spiritual lessons taught in the passage. These would involve your relation to God and to other people; commands to obey; sins to confess and avoid; promises to claim; paths to pursue; warnings to heed.

6. Commentaries and Bible encyclopedias are especially helpful in connection with difficult passages. For such passages, consult the outside sources only after you have spent much time in analyzing the text yourself. (The Notes section of each lesson is intended to throw light on such obscure or difficult passages.)

7. Charts appear throughout this manual, as they do in the entire Self-Study Series.[1] There are two main charts: (1) survey chart, intended to show structure and setting; and (2) analytical chart, representing an analysis of a segment of paragraphs. (See the author's *Independent Bible Study* for a description of these methods.) Study the survey charts to help you see the larger context of each passage. Use the analytical chart work sheets as a place to record your own observations.

8. This manual is divided into ten lessons. However, it is not necessary that each lesson be completed in one sitting, or in one class session. You the student or, in the case of a class situation, the teacher, should decide the length of any one unit of study. Depth—not area—and relaxation—not pressure—are the determining guides here.

9. Lessons based on Scripture portions are divided into six parts, described below:

a. Preparation for study. This section is intended to prepare you for the passage to be analyzed. Setting is one item discussed.

b. Analysis. This is the heart of your independent study. Questions abound, intended to help you observe the important items. Write out all answers. Use the work sheet of an analytical chart whenever possible.

c. Notes. These are explanations and commentaries of important parts of the text, for which outside help is usually needed.

d. Further advanced study. Subjects recommended for study here are usually word or topical studies, involving passages

---

1. This writer wishes to recognize artist Henry Franz for his work in laying out the hundreds of charts in this series.

throughout the Bible. The best outside helps for word studies are an exhaustive concordance (such as Strong's or Young's), and a word study book, such as Vine's (see Bibliography).

e. Applications. Selected questions appear here concerning spiritual lessons of the passage. If you are studying in a group such as a home Bible class, you will want to spend much time discussing such questions.

f. Word to ponder. This is a short quote from the passage of the lesson, intended to inspire continued reflection on the Bible text of James.

10. Leaders of home Bible classes are directed to Albert J. Wollen's paperback *How to Conduct Home Bible Classes* for profitable advice on this effective group method of study. The last paragraph of this book reads:

> Perhaps we will not long have the complete public religious freedom we have so long enjoyed and taken for granted. Should the hour come when we lose this privilege, we could have no greater means of preserving and extending our faith than that of small groups meeting in homes around God's Word.[2]

11. Fortify your study of James's epistle with fervent, believing prayer. And depend always on the illuminating ministry of the Holy Spirit as you open your heart and mind to the words of the text.

12. Read Psalm 119 to prepare your heart for James's New Testament book of Proverbs. Are you a teachable servant of God, willing to be corrected by Him?

2. Albert J. Wollen, *How to Conduct Home Bible Classes* (Wheaton, Ill.: Scripture Press, 1970).

Lesson 1

The Man James

The purpose of this first lesson is to introduce the man James to the readers and students of his epistle. It goes without saying that to know the author is to better understand and appreciate his writing. It is readily admitted that we do not have an abundance of information concerning the man James, but what we do know makes us feel that James is no stranger to us after all.[1] And what is more, Christians know the divine Author of this epistle in an experiential relationship, which is the master key to our understanding its message. (Note: As you study this lesson, be sure to read every Bible verse cited.)

I. PERSONAL NAME

The English name "James" in the New Testament translates the Greek *Iakōbos*. This is a Graecized form of *Iakob*, translated "Jacob" in the New Testament.

II. FAMILY BACKGROUND

To learn something of the author's family background, we first need to identify which James this is. Actually, there are four different New Testament persons with the name James:
James the son of Zebedee (Matt. 4:21; Mark 1:19; Luke 5:10)
James the son of Alphaeus (Matt. 10:3; Mark 3:18; 15:40; Luke 6:15; Acts 1:13)
James the father of Judas the apostle (Luke 6:16, *Berkeley*)
James "the Lord's brother" (Matt. 13:55; Mark 6:3; Gal. 1:19)

---

1. Practically all of our knowledge of James comes from New Testament history. Tradition supplies a few items of interest concerning his life.

There is strong support for the belief that the epistle's author was the last-named James. This is the view followed by this study manual. James really was half brother of Jesus, both having the same mother, Mary, but not the same father. (Joseph was only the *legal* father of Jesus; Jesus was conceived of the Holy Spirit, Matt. 1:20.)

James had sisters and at least three brothers besides Jesus: Joses (Joseph), Simon, and Jude (Matt. 13:55). The home environment in which James was reared must have been an exceptional one, with such devout parents as Mary and Joseph. Yet, the parents could not make their children's decisions concerning belief in Jesus as Saviour and Lord (Messiah). When it was that James made his decision is the subject of the next section.

Whether James ever married and raised his own family is an open question. The only passage in Scripture that may suggest marriage is 1 Corinthians 9:5.

III. CONVERSION

James and the other brothers of Jesus did not believe in Him as Saviour and Lord during the years of Jesus' public ministry. Read John 7:2-8. Does this passage suggest what hindered the brothers from believing? How do you account for this unbelief in light of the fact of such devout upbringing by Mary and Joseph?

_____

_____

What light does Proverbs 22:6 shed on this question?

_____

_____

From Acts 1:14 we learn that James had become a believe sometime before Pentecost day. His conversion may be dated at the time when Jesus appeared to him after His resurrection (1 Cor. 15:7). Or James may have believed just after Jesus' crucifixion. Whenever the experience, it was genuine, for James's entire life was transformed into one of service for Christ, as the book of Acts so clearly reveals.

IV. CHRISTIAN SERVICE

A biography of James's life would show four main periods as indicated by Chart A. Fix this chart clearly in your mind for help in background orientation.

A.D. 27		**30**	**62** Chap. 12
FAMILY RELATIONSHIP TO JESUS HIS BROTHER ①	SPIRITUAL CONFRONTATION WITH JESUS THE MESSIAH ②	CONVERSION ③	WORKER AND LEADER OF THE JERUSALEM CHURCH ④

PERIOD OF THE GOSPELS	Peter the Leader / James the Leader **PERIOD OF THE BOOK OF ACTS**

The third period (conversion) is the shortest and most crucial of the four, representing about fifty days between Jesus' death and Pentecost day (Acts 2).[2] James's ministry as a "servant of God and of the Lord Jesus Christ" (James 1:1) could not begin earlier than his conversion. From his earliest days as a believer, James identified himself with the local Christian group at Jerusalem, praying, working, and serving in various capacities (cf. Acts 1:14). Gradually he was recognized as a leader, so that at least by the time when Peter, the church's key leader during Acts 1-7, left Jerusalem, (Acts 12:17), James was the natural successor. Of this D. A. Hayes writes,

> When he was exalted to this leadership we do not know, but all indications seem to point to the fact that at a very early period James was the recognized executive authority in the church at Jerus, which was the church of Pentecost and the church of the apostles. . . . All Christian Jews would look to Jerus[alem] as the primitive source of their organization and faith, and the head of the church at Jerus[alem] would be recognized by them as their chief authority.[3]

2. The word *pentecost* means fiftieth. Pentecost was the Old Testament Festival of Weeks (cf. Lev. 23:15; Deut. 16:9). The day of Pentecost (Acts 2:1) fell on the fiftieth day after the passion Passover.
3. D.A. Hayes, "Epistle of James," in *The International Standard Bible Encyclopedia* (Grand Rapids: Eerdmans, 1949), 3: 1563. It should be observed here that the book of Acts does not give much information concerning James's leadership during those decades.

9

It was just about this time also that James wrote his epistle, whose content reveals that he was an active Christian worker and leader at the time of writing.

The Bible references shown below reconstruct for us something of the biography of James up to the time of his death. Read all the passages (plus the contexts surrounding them) and record the information furnished by each reference.

During Jesus' public ministry

John 2:12

Matthew 12:46-50

John 7:1-9

Early days as a believer

1 Corinthians 15:7

Early years as a servant of Jesus Christ

Acts 1:14

Galatians 1:18-19 (cf. Acts 9:26)

Successor to Peter as leader of the Jerusalem church

Acts 12:17

Acts 15:13

Galatians 2:1, 9-10 (What is the significance of James's being mentioned first in Paul's list of three pillars, Gal. 2:9-10

V. CHARACTER

The biography of a man is incomplete without a description of his character. Review the verses you have just studied in connection with James's life. Recall, for example, that James was a praying man (Ac. 1:14). One church historian, Hegesippus (c. A.D. 175), commended James's prayer life especially, noting how he spent long hours interceding for the people, so that his knees became calloused.

The best insight into James' character is gained by reading his own writing. Take a few minutes at this point in your study to read the epistle with one object in mind: learning what kind of a man James was. Record your impressions, and compare these with the partial list given here:

a praying man

___

pure

___

powerful

___

practical

___

plain

___

persistent

___

humble

___

honest

___

single-minded

___

just ("fair-minded," "upright," *Berkeley*)

___

Concerning the last-named trait, James came to be known by the early church as "James the Just." It is interesting to note that James's father, Joseph, was "a just man" (Matt. 1:19); and that James refers to Jesus as "the just" man (James 5:6). *The International Standard Bible Encyclopedia* pursues this thought at length, showing how the younger brother James and his elder brother Jesus were so much alike as to personality.[4] The context and style of their messages were similar, as we shall see later in this lesson.

You will learn more about James's character as you analyze carefully the epistle which he was inspired to write. For now, however, try to form a mental image of James's entire life and character on the basis of your studies in this lesson thus far. Whenever necessary, fill in the blank spaces of his biography, with the help of a controlled imagination. When you begin your analytical studies of the text, bring this picture of James with you into your studies, and the Bible text will be more meaningful.

VI. DEATH

A strong tradition is that James was martyred at Jerusalem in A.D. 62. This date is about one year after the closing of the book of Acts and about five years before Paul and Peter were martyred. The manner of death, if Josephus (A.D. 37-95) and others are correct, was by stoning at the order of Ananias the high priest.

Why do you think the New Testament records the deaths of only a few of its main characters?

_____

_____

What spiritual teaching may be learned from this?

_____

_____

VII. REVIEW QUESTIONS

1. Who are the four different New Testament persons with the name James?

_____

_____

4. Ibid., p. 1567.

12

Which one is most likely the author of the epistle?

_____

_____

2. Recall what is known about James's family background.

_____

_____

3. What did James not believe about Jesus during His public ministry?

_____

What may have been the main hindrance?

_____

4. Draw from memory the chart of the periods of James's life.
5. What do you think brought James to believe in Christ?

_____

6. List what is known from the New Testament about James's part in the local Jerusalem church's experience during the thirty years of Acts' history.

_____

_____

_____

7. Describe the personality and character of James.

_____

8. What is traditionally held about James's death?

_____

_____

9. List some important spiritual truths that you have learned in your study of this lesson.

_____

_____

_____

Lesson 2
Background and Survey

James is the man whom God inspired to write what has been called the 'Proverbs of the New Testament.' In this lesson we will inquire into the backgrounds of James's experience in writing such a vibrant epistle. Here we are asking such questions as, What was the particular occasion calling for this letter? What kind of people needed its message? How did it accomplish its purpose? What are its credentials for a place in the Holy Bible?

After we have studied these backgrounds of James's epistle, we will want to make an overall survey of the book, as an introductory study to the detailed analyses of the lessons that follow. Thus our present lesson is of two parts: Background and Survey. If you are studying with a group, it is recommended that you study this lesson in no fewer than two units (e.g., one lesson on background, and one or more lessons on survey).

I. BACKGROUND

A. Author

The Bible text itself identifies the author by name: "James"; and by relationship to God: "servant of God and of the Lord Jesus Christ." In Lesson 1 of this James was identified to be most probably the half brother of Jesus (Mark 6:3; Matt. 13:55; Gal. 1:19).

B. The People Addressed

The salutation identifies the original readers of this letter as "the twelve tribes which are scattered abroad." Like many passages in the Bible, this phrase could be interpreted literally or symbolically.

1. *Literal interpretation:* Were the readers (1) *Jews in general* representing the twelve families of Israel, living in different parts of the New Testament world, of what is usually called the Dispersion *(Diaspora)*; or (2) *Jewish Christians* scattered abroad for various reasons?[1] Read at least part of chapter 1 and see why the first view (Jews in general) is unacceptable.

2. *Symbolic interpretation:* These scattered "twelve tribes" represent the Christian church, God's elect (cf. Gal. 3:7-9; 6:16; Phil. 3:3), living in a strange country (this world), far from their land of citizenship (heaven). (Cf. 1 Pet. 1:1, 17; 2:11; Phil. 3:20; Gal. 4:26; Heb. 12:22; 13:14.)

The contents of the epistle itself strongly support the view that James's readers were *Jewish Christians*, wherever they were located. This would be expected, if the epistle was written at a very early date (see Date below), for most Christians in the earliest days were Jews (cf. Acts 1-7).

Indications in the epistle itself that James's readers were Jews include these (read the verses):

1. the reference to "synagogue" ("assembly," KJV), not "church" (2:2)[2]

2. illustrations from the Old Testament (e.g., 2:25; 5:11, 17)

3. the reference to Abraham as "our father" (2:21)

4. the Old Testament name "Lord of sabaoth" (5:4)

5. no mention of what might be called "pagan" vices, such as idolatry and drunkenness.

C. Date and Place Written

The position of this study manual is that James was the earliest (or one of the earliest) New Testament books to be written. (See Chart D.) The date of writing was around A.D. 45-50.

Associate the writing of James with the times of the book of Acts, with the help of Chart B, a condensed survey chart of Acts:[3]

The view of a later date places the writing of James around A.D. 60, a year or so before James's death.[4] Reasons for the early date include:

1. *Diaspora* is the Greek word translated "scattered abroad" in 1:1. Persecutions dating back as far as the Assyrian captivity (721 B.C.) and pursuit of commerce accounted for most of this "dispersion."
2. The word "church" does appear, however, in 5:14.
3. From Irving L. Jensen, *Acts: An Inductive Study* (Chicago: Moody, 1968), p. 52.
4. Some hold to a late date on such grounds as: James 2:14-26 was written to correct a misinterpretation of Paul's doctrine of justification by faith contained in such writings as Romans (c. A.D. 56); and references to persecutions fit a late date better than an early date.

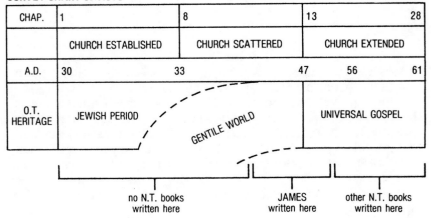

CHAP.	1	8	13	28
	CHURCH ESTABLISHED	CHURCH SCATTERED	CHURCH EXTENDED	

A.D.	30	33	47	56	61

O.T. HERITAGE	JEWISH PERIOD	GENTILE WORLD	UNIVERSAL GOSPEL

no N.T. books written here   JAMES written here   other N.T. books written here

1. Church order and discipline in the epistle are simple.

2. The Jerusalem Council of Acts 15 (A.D. 48 or 49) was still future: "The question of the admission of the Gentiles [into the church, which in the earliest years was Jewish] seems not yet to have come to the fore."[5]

3. The Judaic emphases on law, moral principles, and works were the immediate concerns of the first decades of the church.

As to the question of the place of writing James, it is very probable that James was living in Palestine when he wrote the epistle.

D. Occasion

Persecution of the Christians, unchristian conduct (e.g., in speech) by many believers, and erroneous views on such doctrines as faith and sin were some of the circumstances that called for this epistle.

E. Purpose

Most of the epistle was written to correct evils and to teach right Christian behavior. There are also encouragement and exhortation in things such as the coming of the Lord (e.g., 5:7). The epistle has been called "A Practical Guide to Christian Life and Con-

---

5. Henry C. Thiessen, *Introduction to the New Testament* (Grand Rapids: Eerdmans, 1943), p. 277.

17

duct." More of James's purposes will be observed in the Survey study of this lesson.

F. Contents

James emphasizes *conduct* more than *creed*. For this reason James has been called the apostle of good works, an identification linking him with the trio of John, apostle of love; Paul, apostle of faith; and Peter, apostle of hope. There is little of systematically presented theology in the book. Specific references to Jesus and the gospel are few, though this does not take away from the Christian spirit that pervades the book.[6] On this, D.A. Hayes writes, "James says less about the Master than any other writer in the New Testament, but his speech is more like that of the Master than the speech of any of them."[7]

A comparison of the book of James with Jesus' Sermon on the Mount shows an extraordinary likeness. Read the parallel verses listed on page 16, and record the common teaching for each set.

Because of the nature of James's message, many different subjects are treated in the epistle. Some of these are: patience, prayer, love, liberty, equality, humility, peace, steadfastness, self-control, and wisdom. Other subjects will appear in our survey and analytical studies.

G. Comparison with Other Books

Some interesting comparisons between James and other parts of Scripture are suggested below. You may want to inquire more into this subject at a later time.

1. *Proverbs of the Old Testament.* James and Proverbs are both concerned primarily with *conduct*.

2. *Jesus' Sermon on the Mount.* These comparisons were made above.

3. *Paul's writings (especially Galatians and Romans).* The most obvious observation to be made here is a difference of emphasis: Paul emphasizes the place of faith, and James the place of works. There is no contradiction here, however, though some

---

6. The two verses containing the name "Jesus" are 1:1 and 2:1. The name "Lord" occurs fifteen times in the epistle.
7. D.A. Hayes, "Epistle of James," in *International Standard Bible Encyclopedia,*, 3:1564.

Sermon on the Mount	James	Common Teaching
Matthew 5:48	James 1:4	COMPLETION AND PERFECTION
7:7	1:5	SEEK AND ASK AND IT WILL be GIVEN
Mark 11:23	1:6	HAVE FAITH DO NOT DOUBT
Matthew 7:24, 26	1:22	BE A DOER OF THE WORD
John 13:17	1:25	BE A DOER OF THE WORKS AND WORD
Luke 6:20	2:5	BLESSED ARE THE POOR
6:24-25	5:1	MISERIES WILL COME UPON THE RICH AND PROUD
Matthew 7:1	4:11-12	DO NOT JUDGE OTHERS
5:34-37	5:12	DO NOT SWEAR BY HEAVEN or EARTH
7:16-20	3:12	KNOW OTHERS BY THEIR FRUIT

theologians have concluded so.[8] The difference between the two books is accounted for by the fact of two different vantage points. Paul deals with "Justification Before God," James, "Demonstration Before men." "Paul saw Christ in the heavens, establishing our righteousness. James saw Him on the earth, telling us to be perfect...."[9]

Refer to Chart C for comparisons of the various New Testament books. Note especially how James and Galatians are compared, thus:

GALATIANS: Liberation by the gospel
JAMES: Compulsion of the gospel

8. The notable example of refuting James is that of Martin Luther, who wrote that James "contradicts Paul and all Scriptures, seeking to accomplish by enforcing the law what the apostles successfully effect by love" (quoted by Hayes, p. 1566.)
9. Henrietta C. Mears, *What the Bible Is All About* (Glendale, Calif.: Gospel Light, 1953), p. 595.

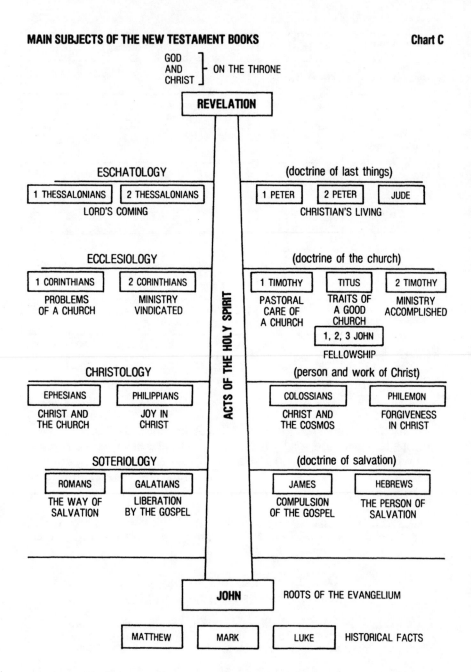

GOD AND CHRIST] ON THE THRONE

REVELATION

ESCHATOLOGY (doctrine of last things)

| 1 THESSALONIANS | 2 THESSALONIANS | 1 PETER | 2 PETER | JUDE |

LORD'S COMING CHRISTIAN'S LIVING

ECCLESIOLOGY (doctrine of the church)

| 1 CORINTHIANS | 2 CORINTHIANS | 1 TIMOTHY | TITUS | 2 TIMOTHY |

PROBLEMS OF A CHURCH MINISTRY VINDICATED PASTORAL CARE OF A CHURCH TRAITS OF A GOOD CHURCH MINISTRY ACCOMPLISHED

1, 2, 3 JOHN

FELLOWSHIP

ACTS OF THE HOLY SPIRIT

CHRISTOLOGY (person and work of Christ)

| EPHESIANS | PHILIPPIANS | COLOSSIANS | PHILEMON |

CHRIST AND THE CHURCH JOY IN CHRIST CHRIST AND THE COSMOS FORGIVENESS IN CHRIST

SOTERIOLOGY (doctrine of salvation)

| ROMANS | GALATIANS | JAMES | HEBREWS |

THE WAY OF SALVATION LIBERATION BY THE GOSPEL COMPULSION OF THE GOSPEL THE PERSON OF SALVATION

JOHN ROOTS OF THE EVANGELIUM

| MATTHEW | MARK | LUKE | HISTORICAL FACTS

A study of this chart is one good way to survey the main content of the New Testament.

4. *Other general epistles.*

James and 1 Peter—predominantly ethical (Christian behavior)
Jude and 2 Peter—eschatological (doctrine of last events)
Epistles of John—Christological and ethical

It is interesting to observe that James, the first author of the New Testament, and John, the last author, both write with a note of authority, emphasizing conduct acceptable to God.

H. Style

The book of James is a letter, as its salutation indicates, but its style is more like that of a preacher's sermon or an Old Testament prophet's appeal. James writes in simple, straightforward sentences. Like Old Testament writings and Jesus' discourses, there are no abstractions, and picture language abounds. Most of the sixty-three Greek words unique to James's letter are picture words, such as "poison," "fade." The epistle bristles with strong, pointed truths from the first word to the last. Hayes says of James, "He has the dramatic instinct. He has the secret of sustained interest . . . .He is an artist."[10]

I. Tone

A tone of authority pervades the epistle. (There are 54 imperatives in the 108 verses.) For this, James has been called "The Amos of the New Testament." But James's forthrightness and severity are blended with warmth and love, evidenced by the repeated words "brethren" and "beloved brethren." Read 1:5, 17; 2:5; 4:6 and 5:11, 19, 20 for some of the more tender sentences of the epistle.

J. Place in the Canon

Questions over authorship and doctrine delayed general recognition of this book's divine inspiration, but as of the end of the fourth century the epistle of James was firmly fixed in the canon of Holy Scriptures. The book is usually classified as a general epistle, the designation referring to destination (e.g., a group not identified with one city), contents, or both.

10. Hayes, p. 1564.

K. Summary

Thus far we have spent a fair amount of time studying the background of the epistle of James. This is important for a full appreciation of why and how the epistle was written in the first place. Through knowing such things, we have more incentive and direction to relate the two-thousand-year-old message to our contemporary scene. The remainder of this study manual is devoted to the actual text which communicates this message.

II. SURVEY

Now let us go to the text of James itself, which is the main object of our study. The best procedure, as in all Bible study, is first to make a survey, or "skyscraper" view, of the book in general, before moving to the analytical studies which begin with Lesson 3.

As you make your own survey of James, keep from getting involved in details, which is the task of analysis. Look especially for *main emphasis* and *broad movements*.

A. A First Reading

Scan the book in one sitting, reading aloud if possible. You may choose to do this first in a modern paraphrase or version and then in the version of your study.

What are your first impressions of the book?

_____

_____

What things stand out?

_____

_____

B. Subsequent Readings

1. Scan the book again, underlining every appearance of the address "my brethren" (or related phrases). How often is this repeated? Is there any pattern as to where the phrase appears?

_____

_____

_____

BOOK	AUTHOR	PLACE WRITTEN	DATE A.D.	PERIODS		
				Personnel	Apostolic Literature	Church
James	– James	Jerusalem	45			
Galatians			48			
1 Thessalonians		Corinth	52			
2 Thessalonians	– Paul			FIRST PAULINE PERIOD	BEGINNINGS –about 15 years	FOUNDING
1 Corinthians		Ephesus	55			
2 Corinthians		Macedonia				
Romans		Corinth	56			
Matthew	– Matthew	Jerusalem?		FIRST HISTORICAL RECORDS		
Luke	– Luke	Rome	61			
Acts						
Colossians				CENTRAL PAULINE PERIOD		
Ephesians	– Paul	Rome	61			
Philemon						
Philippians						
1 Timothy			62	PAUL'S LEGACY	CENTRAL –about 10 years	ESTABLISHING
Titus	– Paul	Rome				
2 Timothy			67			
Hebrews	– ?					
Jude	– Jude					
1 Peter				PETER'S LEGACY		
2 Peter	– Peter		68?			
Mark	– Mark					
FALL OF JERUSALEM A.D. 70					15 "silent" years	
John		Ephesus?	85			
1 John				JOHN'S LEGACY	CLOSING –about 10 years	CONTINUING
2 John	– John					
3 John						
Revelation		Patmos	96			

23

What does this brief study tell you about the epistle?

_____

2. Compare the opening verses (e.g., 1:1-4) with the closing verses (e.g., 5:19-20).

_____

_____

3. With a pencil, mark paragraph divisions in your Bible at these places: 1:1, 2, 5, 9, 13, 16, 19, 22, 26; 2:1, 5, 8, 14, 18, 19, 21, 25; 3:1, 3, 5*b*, 7, 9, 13; 4:1, 4, 11, 13; 5:1, 7, 13, 19.

4. Now read each paragraph, and derive a strong word or phrase (no longer than three words) from each paragraph that is a clue to its content. Record these on Chart E. (See examples shown. Note: Each reference on the chart is the opening verse of the particular paragraph.)

5. Observe in the epistle every reference to each of the subjects listed below. (Underline these in your Bible in a methodical way, such as using one color for one subject, another color for another subject, and so forth. This will be of great assistance to you now and in your later analyses.)

    a. references to God, Jesus, Lord

    b. use of questions

    c. specific references to the Old Testament

    d. figurative language (e.g., "vapour," 4:14)

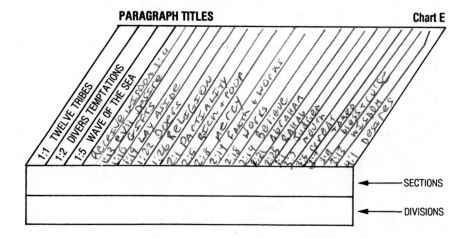

PARAGRAPH TITLES   Chart E

SECTIONS

DIVISIONS

6. Record a list of key words and phrases for James on the basis of your study thus far. Compare your list with that shown on the survey Chart G.

C. Observing the Structure of the Epistle

So far we have been engaged in observing big individual items in James's letter, with no inquiry into how these different parts are brought together into one whole. So search for structure is our present task.

There are various ways one may record a study of the structure of a book of the Bible. A survey chart (e.g., Chart G) is one such way. Try making at least a simple survey chart for James, showing a main outline for the epistle. You yourself will have to determine how much time you can devote to this study. In any case, learn the survey Chart G before doing the analytical lessons which begin with Lesson 3.

If you choose to construct a survey chart on your own, here are suggested procedures.

1. Review the paragraph titles which you recorded on Chart E. Read the epistle again, and identify *groups* of paragraphs according to *common* subject. (Let us call such a group of paragraphs a section; and a group of sections, a division.) For example, what paragraphs speak about the common subject of the tongue (speech)? Mark on Chart E, in the first blank space for sections, where this and other groups of paragraph appear. This may be the most difficult part of your study in James because this epistle is not a formal treatise as such, but a series of exhortations written in a pattern whose order is not apparent, for the most part. So do not become discouraged if you cannot identify many groups of paragraphs. At the same time, do not leave this phase of study prematurely. Take on the challenge of finding an outline, as obscure as one may appear. That is how discoveries are often born. An example of this is the testimony of J. Albrecht Bengel concerning his study of the maxims of Proverbs:

> I have often been in such an attitude of soul, that those chapters in the Book of Proverbs in which I had before looked for no connection whatever, presented themselves to me as if the proverbs belonged in the most beautiful order one with another.[11]

11. Quoted in John Peter Lange, *Commentary on the Holy Scriptures: Proverbs* (Grand Rapids: Zondervan, n.d.), p. 33.

It may be added here that any time spent in search of structure of a book of the Bible is not lost time, for its fruits keep reappearing in the later stages of analytical study.

2. The next logical step in determining the structure of a book is to identify divisions, which are of sections. Record your findings in the appropriate space of Chart E. Three outlines by different authors are shown on Chart F as examples of various ways in which the structure of James has been outlined.[12] Compare these also with the survey Chart G.

VARIOUS OUTLINES OF JAMES   **Chart F**

1:1	2:1	3:1	4:1	5:1

①

		3:13		5:19
NATURE OF TRUE RELIGION	NATURE OF TRUE FAITH	NATURE OF TRUE WISDOM		PURPOSE OF WISDOM

②

LIVING FAITH TESTED BY TRIAL	LIVING FAITH PROVED BY WORKS	LIVING FAITH EVIDENCED BY CONDUCT	LIVING FAITH EXERCISED BY PERSECUTION

③

			4:13
TEST OF FAITH	NATURE OF FAITH	WORKS OF FAITH	APPLICATION OF FAITH

3. A survey chart should also show turning points, introduction, and conclusion whenever these are present in the text. A title for the book can also usually be determined at this point of study.

Whether or not you have worked on your own survey chart, study carefully survey Chart G. Observe the following:

1. There is a formal salutation in James, but no formal closing.

2. The bottom of the chart shows four main divisions in the epistle. There is an ascending progression in the first three: "Principles Involved;" "Practices for the Present;" "Prizes in the Future." The fourth section is like an epilogue, where the writer re-

12. These are outlines, respectively, of (1) Merrill C. Tenney, *New Testament Survey* (Grand Rapids: Eerdman, 1961), pp. 263-64; (2) Merrill F. Unger, *Unger's Bible Handbook* (Chicago: Moody, 1966), p. 784; (3) Walter M. Dunnett, *An Outline of New Testament Survey* (Chicago: Moody, n.d.), pp. 143-44.

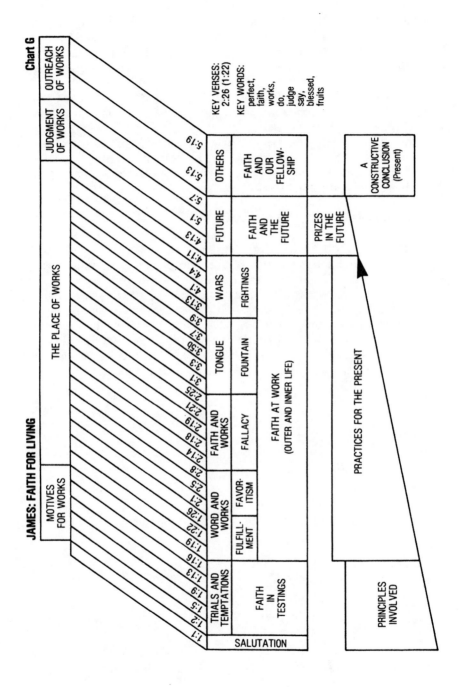

JAMES: FAITH FOR LIVING

Chart G

| MOTIVES FOR WORKS | THE PLACE OF WORKS | JUDGMENT OF WORKS | OUTREACH OF WORKS |

KEY VERSES: 2:26 (1:22)

KEY WORDS: perfect, faith, works, do, judge say, blessed, fruits

| TRIALS AND TEMPTATIONS | WORD AND WORKS | FAITH AND WORKS | TONGUE | WARS | FUTURE | OTHERS |

| FAITH IN TESTINGS | FULFILL-MENT | FAVOR-ITISM | FALLACY | FOUNTAIN | FIGHTINGS | FAITH AND THE FUTURE | FAITH AND OUR FELLOW-SHIP |

FAITH AT WORK (OUTER AND INNER LIFE)

PRIZES IN THE FUTURE

PRACTICES FOR THE PRESENT

A CONSTRUCTIVE CONCLUSION (Present)

PRINCIPLES INVOLVED

SALUTATION

1:1 1:2 1:5 1:9 1:13 1:16 1:19 1:22 1:26 2:1 2:5 2:8 2:14 2:18 2:19 2:21 2:25 3:1 3:3 3:5b 3:7 3:9 3:13 4:1 4:4 4:11 4:13 5:1 5:7 5:13 5:19

27

turns to the subject of "Practices for the Present" by giving two final exhortations of a very practical nature to his Christian readers.

3. Observe how the epistle is first divided into small sections (first outline under the main horizontal line). Then study the outline of large divisions. Check out the outlines with your own observations of the epistle which you have made.

4. The title for James given on the chart is "Faith for Living." The intention of this title is to show the necessary ingredient of *faith* in *action*.[13] This very clearly is James's main theme. The key verse chosen for the epistle (2:26) reflects this theme.

5. Compare the list of key words with those which you have chosen in your study.

III. SUMMARY OF LESSONS 1 and 2

All of our studies thus far in this manual have been intended to prepare us for the *main* task of a comprehensive analysis of the text of James. We have been introduced to the man James, and we have seen what kind of person he is. We have inquired into the backgrounds of the epistle, such as the reasons for its being written in the first place. And we have made a skyscraper view of the epistle in general, to orient our thinking so that we will always be conscious of the forest as we move among the individual trees. The text waits to be analyzed. Let us take up the challenge, with great anticipation.

---

13. Cf. the title of G. Coleman Luck's commentary in the Everyman's Bible Commentary series, *James, Faith in Action.*

Lesson 3

Man's Tests and God's Gifts

We move now into the heart of our study of James, involving analysis, which is the microscopic view. In contrast to survey, which is making a sweeping view of large things, analysis is distinguished by its minute examination of details. Analysis scrutinizes every part, however small, and the relation between them.

There are only five chapters in James, which is an encouragement in itself to study the epistle slowly and carefully. Our present lesson concerns 1:1-18, a unit of study to which we are assigning the title "Man's Tests and God's Gifts."

I. PREPARATION FOR STUDY

1. Try to picture the pressure of persecution burdening the Jewish Christians to whom James wrote this letter. The fact that the first subject referred to in the letter is the hardship of trials, tells us that this was a most pressing problem. Compare a similar passage in 1 Peter 1:6-9.

2. Because the words *temptation* and *trying* ("tried") are key words in this passage, it will help to know what the words mean, by noting how they are used in various New Testament passages. Read all the verses cited below.

   a. Temptation: The Greek word is *peirasmos* and has two basic meanings:[1]

   (1) Trials from without, with a beneficial purpose and effect

   (a) Divinely permitted or sent (James 1:2, 12; Luke 22:28; Acts 20:19; 1 Pet. 1:6; 4:12; 2 Pet. 2:9)

   (b) With a good or neutral significance (Gal. 4:14)

---

1. A third usage of the word is found in Heb. 3:8, where it is used of man's *challenge* of God. See W.E. Vine, *An Expository Dictionary of New Testament Words.* 4:117.

(c) Of a varied character (Matt. 6:13; Luke 11:4; Matt. 26:41; Mark 14:38; Luke 22:40, 46; 1 Cor. 10:13).

(2) Trials from within, definitely designed to lead to wrong doing, such as the kind of temptation referred to in James 1:13-14 (Luke 4:13; 8:13; 1 Tim. 6:9).

B. Trial: The basic meaning of the Greek root *dokime* is "experience." There are two meanings:

(1) The *process* of proving (2 Cor. 8:2)

(2) The *effect* of proving, or *approval*, where the end, not the process, is in view (Rom. 5:4)

On the basis of the above study, interpret this passage of 1 Peter which has both Greek words placed side by side:

> Ye are in heaviness through manifold temptations [*peirasmois*]: that the trial [*dokimion*] of your faith . . . might be found unto praise . . . (1 Pet. 1:6*a*-7*a*).

In determining which alternate meaning of a particular word is intended by the author, context is one of the best clues. This is the reason for the insistence in Bible study of a recognition of how words and phrases relate to each other in their context.

3. Chart H is an excerpt from Chart G, given here as a reminder of the context of our present passage. Why would James want to talk first about faith in testings?

EXCERPT FROM CHART G **Chart H**

1:1	1:19	4:13	5:13 5:20
FAITH IN TESTINGS	FAITH AT WORK	FAITH AND THE FUTURE	FAITH AND OUR FELLOWSHIP
principles involved	practices for the present	prizes in the future	a constructive conclusion

II. ANALYSIS

Segment to be analyzed: 1:1-18
Paragraph divisions: 1, 2, 5, 9, 13, 16

1	twelve tribes

2

5

9

13

16

18

GIFTS FROM ABOVE
JAMES 1:1-18

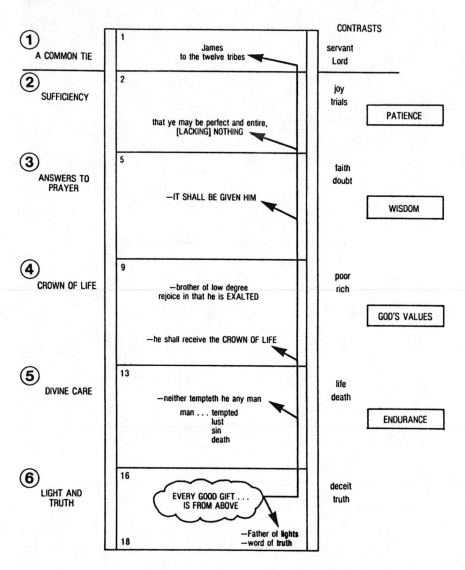

CONTRASTS

(1) A COMMON TIE

1 — James to the twelve tribes — servant / Lord

(2) SUFFICIENCY

2 — joy / trials

that ye may be perfect and entire, [LACKING] NOTHING

PATIENCE

(3) ANSWERS TO PRAYER

5 — faith / doubt

—IT SHALL BE GIVEN HIM

WISDOM

(4) CROWN OF LIFE

9 — poor / rich

—brother of low degree rejoice in that he is EXALTED

—he shall receive the CROWN OF LIFE

GOD'S VALUES

(5) DIVINE CARE

13 — life / death

—neither tempteth he any man

man . . . tempted
lust
sin
death

ENDURANCE

(6) LIGHT AND TRUTH

16 — deceit / truth

EVERY GOOD GIFT . . . IS FROM ABOVE

—Father of lights
—word of truth

18

As you begin your analytical studies in James, you will want to follow routines and study habits that will encourage you to see all that James is writing in these verses. There are various methods of Bible study, and you will want to follow the ones best suited to you. Whatever methods you use, be sure to use pencil and paper to record your observations and conclusions. "The pencil is one of the best eyes!" Suggestions given below are to help you look for things in the Bible text. Let these be starters for study. If you are studying with a group, don't hesitate to discuss at length any one subject, if need be.

Chart I is a work sheet where you may record your observations as you study this passage paragraph by paragraph. Use the space inside the boxes to record words and phrases of the Bible text. Record your own words (e.g., outlines) in the margins. Chart J shows how different kinds of observations may be recorded on the work sheet (which we shall also call an analytical chart).

A. General Analysis

1. Read the passage (1:1-18) in your study version, underlying key words and phrases as you read. Check back with your paragraph titles that you made in Lesson 2. Record the paragraph titles on Chart I (see example shown, "twelve tribes"). Record below *a theme* for each paragraph (that is, what is the main teaching of each paragraph?):

1:1 _____

1:2-4 _____

1:5-8 _____

1:9-12 _____

1:13-15 _____

1:16-18 _____

2. Observe all the places where trials or temptations are referred to in the passage. Is there suggestion of trial in any of the third, fourth or last paragraphs? (We will pursue this subject of trial and temptation in more detail later.)

3. The word "greeting" of 1:1 is translated literally as "rejoice." Follow this subject of *joy* throughout the passage. How is it an inspiring setting for the subject of trials and temptations?

_____

_____

33

What spiritual lessons are taught by this?

_____

_____

4. Look for at least one set of contrasts in each paragraph of the passage. Record this in the margin of your work sheet.
5. Observe at least one good Christian trait in each of the paragraphs. Record.
6. What do you think is the one main truth that James is establishing in this passage?

_____

_____

7. Do you see any other subjects referred to in the segment from paragraph to paragraph?

_____

_____

8. Study the analytical Chart J and note the following:
_a._ A topical study with the title "Gifts from Above."
Where is this title derived from?

_____

_____

Note the six paragraph points under this title. What phrase in the text does each point represent?

_____

_____

_____

_b._ Contrasts in each paragraph.
_c._ Good Christian virtues. Add to the list during your study.

B. Paragraph Analysis

Now let us move to the smaller unit, the paragraph, and analyze each one in detail. Involved here, of course, is the study of sentences (verses), phrases, and words.
1. _Paragraph 1:1_
How is James identified?

_____

_____

How are the twelve tribes identified?

_____

One relates to status in ministry: the other relates to circumstances in status. What does the phrase "twelve tribes" represent?

_____

What circumstance is suggested by "scattered abroad" (lit. "in the
dispersion")?

_____

What were the common ties between James and his readers?

_____

What was the most important one?

_____

James seems proud to be called a servant (lit. "bondslave") of God
and of the Lord. Other leaders in the church were of the same
mind (cf. Rom. 1:1; 2 Pet. 1:1; Rev. 1:1). Account for this satisfaction
of such a relationship.

_____

What distinction may James have had in mind in naming the two
Persons of the Godhead to whom he gave allegiance in servitude:
God

_____

Lord Jesus Christ

_____

What truth about the Son of God is represented by each of these
designations (see Notes for the derivation of these):
the title "Christ":

_____

_____

the name "Jesus" (cf. Matt. 1:21):

_____

_____

the title "Lord" (Can Jesus be Lord without being Saviour, and vise versa?):

_____

_____

How is the word "greeting" (lit. "rejoice") a clue to the overall purpose of James in writing this letter?

_____

_____

Read Acts 15:23 and note this same salutation used by the Jerusalem church over which James presided.

2. *Paragraph 1:2-4*

First, observe the progression in the life of a believer, beginning with the situation of temptations:

> temptations v. 2—The situation
> trying v. 3*a*—The test
> patience vv. 3*b*, 4*a*—The immediate fruit
> maturity "perfect" v. 4*b*—The ultimate fruit

Study this progression in the light of the comparative study of the words "temptation" and "trial" that was made earlier in the lesson. Also, keep in mind that the phrase "fall into . . . temptations" does not mean *yielding* to temptations but *encountering* the challenge of temptations. Compare modern versions on this phrase (e.g., NASB* uses the word "encounter"). Would it be correct to say that James's reference to "temptations" here, in view of the setting of the epistle, was to tribulations, such as persecution, from without?

Apply the following definition of "trying" to verse 3: Trying is a *proving* with the view to *approving*. Can one learn patience without experience of tests? Is patience merely a passive and static endurance in circumstances, or a dynamic progress to a goal involved? Why is patience such an important Christian virtue? Compare Romans 5:3-5.

_____

_____

New American Standard Bible.

How was Christ the supreme example of patience (cf. Heb. 12:2)?

_____

_____

What is the ultimate benefit that comes to the believer who is victorious in the process of verses 2-4?

_____

_____

Is this blessing only a reward to be received in the distant future, or is it attainable in the daily life of the believer? Explain.

_____

_____

The phrase "wanting nothing" (better, "lacking nothing") defines the word "entire." In what sense does the victorious believer described in these verses lack nothing?

_____

_____

The word "perfect" of verse 4 has in it the idea of maturity, full-grown stature. (See Notes.) Compare Ephesians 4:13 and Colossians 4:12 in various modern versions. The word does not mean sinless.
On the basis of your analysis of these verses, explain why James can open the paragraph with the bright words "count it all joy."

_____

_____

3. *Paragraph 1:5-8*
Compare the first phrase of this paragraph ("But if you lack wisdom") with the last of the previous paragraph ("lacking nothing").[2] What is the thought involved?

_____

_____

Compare also the references to faith in each of these two paragraphs: "trying of your faith" (v. 3); "ask in faith" (v. 6). Why is faith basic to Christian living?

_____

_____

2. The addition of the word "but" is a preferred reading of the Greek text.

(Note: Now is a good time to begin recording in permanent form all the truths taught about faith in the epistle of James. Recall our title for James—"Faith for Living.")
The situation of need (problem) of 1:2-4 is what?

_____

_____

What is it in this paragraph (1:5-8)?

_____

_____

What is heart wisdom?

_____

_____

Compare it with head knowledge.[3] Read such verses as 1 Kings 3:9ff; Psalm 111:10; James 3:13, 15, 17. Name some areas of Christian living today where there is special need of wisdom from God.

_____

_____

_____

If a Christian lacks wisdom in any area, does God reproach him for it?

_____

What is the condition imposed upon man for receiving wisdom from "the giving God" (literal translation in place of "the God that giveth")?

_____

_____

What different adjectives (most of them picture words) in verses 6-8 describe the Christian lacking in faith? Record these, and tell what each means:
v. 6

_____

_____

_____

3. Sometimes in the Old Testament the words "wisdom" and "knowledge" are used interchangeably (e.g., Prov. 2:3-6). When that is the case, the "knowledge" is not mere head knowledge but heart discernment.

v. 8

_____

What is the tragic presumption of verse 7?

_____

How does this describe many Christians today?

_____

How does your prayer life measure up to these words:
"Ask in faith, nothing wavering"?

_____

What do you think James means by "a double minded man" (v. 8)
in the context of prayer?

_____

We have already observed a note of joy in the first two paragraphs
of this segment. Although there is no specific reference to joy in
this paragraph, there is a very bright note. What is it?

_____

4. *Paragraph 1:9-12*
The word "rejoice" (v. 9) is better translated in the strong form,
"glory" (see various versions). The presence of this verb is implied after the word "rich" in verse 10. The "rich" of verse 10 are
wealthy Christians; then to whom does the contrasting phrase
"brother of low degree" refer?

_____

In what sense is the financially poor Christian man exalted?

_____

_____

Do you think that many of James's readers had experienced the trial of poverty? If so, could this be the reason for the inclusion of this paragraph at this point?

_____

Study verses 10-12 carefully to learn why a wealthy Christian can glory in being "made low."
a. What three things are said to happen to such a rich man:

_____ (10a);

_____ (10b);

_____ (11b)?

b. What is said about each of the following:
grass

_____

flower

_____

grace of its fashion ("lovely appearance," Berkeley)

_____

c. What trial brings about these consequences to the plant?

_____

d. What trial in the experience of a wealthy Christian does this illustrate?

_____

What then is intended by the phrase "he is made low"?

_____

e. Is this parabolic illustration intended to be applied word for word? That is, are we to conclude that a trial involving a Christian's wealth will bring death to the man himself? If not, what is brought to death?

_____

Correct answers to these questions will be the natural explanation to the original problem of how a wealthy Christian can glory in being made low.

40

f. Observe how verse 12, included as the last verse of this paragraph,[4] gives a strong and clear answer to the wealthy Christian's victory over the lure of material things:

He loves the Lord (not money).
He perseveres in the testing ("endureth temptation").
His reward is a crown of life.

5. *Paragraph 1:13-15*

This paragraph is about two different views as to the source of temptation: a false view and a correct one. Record the two views below:

v. 13

_____

vv. 14-15

_____

What kind of temptation is the subject here: temptation (trial) from without, or temptation (luring) from within? How does your answer agree with the last phrase of verse 13, "neither tempteth he any man"?)

_____

What would make a person blame God for sending temptations his way?

_____

Did God cause Adam and Eve to sin the first sins of the human race? What consolation is there to all people, saved and unsaved alike, that temptations to sin do not have their origin from above?

_____

How does verse 14 identify where the experience of being tempted has its source?

_____

_____

4. Most Bible versions print v. 12 as the beginning of the next paragraph. But this verse is about temptation from without, whereas vv. 13-15 are about the luring type of temptation from within. *The New Bible Commentary* sees v. 12 as a natural conclusion to vv. 9-11.

Study the following progression of verses 14-15:

lust in the heart	(sin nature)
drawn away (enticed)	(the situation)
sin	(the sinful act)
death	(the consequences)

What awesome truths are taught by these few words: "Sin, when it is finished, bringeth forth death" (v. 15*b*)?

_____

_____

6. Paragraph 1:16-18.
The paragraph opens with a simple, general command: "Do not err." Compare this with the personal opening commands or exhortations of the previous four paragraphs:
  "My brethren, count it all joy" (v. 2)
  "If any of you lack wisdom, let him ask of God" (v. 5)
  "Let the brother of low degree rejoice" (v. 9)
  "Let no man say . . . I am tempted of God" (v. 13)
Show how verse 16 could be a transitional verse, referring to the subject of SOURCE in the paragraph before it and in the verses that follow. Record your conclusions:

vv. 13-15			SOURCE:
v. 16—	"Do	not	err"
vv. 17-18			SOURCE:

What are the bright words of this paragraph? What precious truths for the believer are suggested by each?

_____

_____

How is God identified in the paragraph?

_____

_____

What do you think is meant by these phrases:
"begat he us with the word of truth" (v. 18)

_____

_____

"firstfruits of his creatures" (v. 18)

_____

_____

C. Summary of 1:1-18

Think back over your analysis of this segment and list at least one important truth written about the following subjects in each paragraph:

Paragraph	TESTINGS and TEMPTATIONS	GIFTS FROM GOD
1:1		
1:2-4	PROVING PRODUCES ENDURANCE	JOY
1:5-8	DO NOT DOUBT	WISDOM
1:9-12	rich vs. poor	HUMILITY
1:13-15	GOD DOES NOT TEMPT	HE TEMPTS NO ONE
1:16-18		EVERY GOOD AND PERFECT GIFT

III. NOTES

1. "Lord Jesus Christ" (1:1). Each designation of Christ has a special significance. In Jesus' day the common title "lord" *(kurios)* was applied to various persons, such as (1) an owner (Luke 19:33); (2) a master (Matt. 6:24); (3) an emperor or king (Acts 25:26); (4) idols (1 Cor. 8:5); (5) a father (Matt. 21:30); (6) a stranger, out of courtesy (John 12:21). The title *Lord* as applied to God was one of the most frequent Old Testament titles (a concordance shows

thousands of Old Testament references). Jesus Himself assumed the title true to His divine calling. On this, Hogg and Vine write:

> His purpose did not become clear to the disciples until after His resurrection, and the revelation of His Deity consequent thereon. Thomas, when he realized the significance of the presence of a mortal wound in the body of a living man, immediately joined with it the absolute title of Deity, saying, "My Lord and my God," John 20:28. Thereafter, except in Acts 10:4 and Rev. 7:14, there is no record that *kurios* was ever again used by believers in addressing any save God and the Lord Jesus: cp. Acts 2:47 with 4:29, 30.[5]

The name "Jesus" was Christ's personal name. Read Matthew 1:21. It is a transliteration of the Hebrew *Jeshua* (Joshua) meaning "Jehovah is salvation."

The title "Christ" is derived from *krino* ("anoint") and thus means "the anointed one."

2. "Fall into . . . temptations" (1:2). The word "fall" does not have the connotation of yielding to a sinful desire but of encountering a circumstance that surrounds the person. Compare Luke 10:30 where it is said that the traveler to Jericho *"fell among thieves."* This is the same word used in James 1:2.

3. "Perfect and entire" (1:4). The word "perfect" denotes "that which has reached its maturity or fulfilled the end contemplated."[6] The word "entire" means having all which properly belongs to the subject, literally, "entire allotment." The same word is translated "perfect soundness" in Acts 3:16 (read this verse).

4. "If any of you lack wisdom" (1:5). The context leading up to this verse is the situation of trials. It seems as though James anticipates all kinds of questions about trials—why, how, what, wherefore, and so on. So now he says, "For your answers, go to God." The literal translation of the phrase in verse 5 is "Ask of the giving God."

5. "Liberally" (1:5). The word means "simply." Compare Romans 12:8. This kind of giving is not marred by such things as wrong motives, evil attitudes, and restricted dimensions.

6. "Drawn away of [by] his own lust, and enticed" (1:14). James may have had especially in mind temptations to immoral acts when he wrote verses 13-15. If so, it is important for us to observe the unexpanded extent of his (and other Bible writers') trea-

---

5. Quoted by Vine, 3: 17.
6. Marvin R. Vincent, *Word Studies in the New Testament*, 1: 724.

tise on sex education. This subject of sex education, a vital issue in American life today, is not new. Decades ago A.T. Robertson wrote:

> One is reminded afresh of the opening chapters of Proverbs, which cannot be excelled by any of the modern books on sex instruction, some of which stimulate more immorality than they prevent. Wise warning is needed and plain talk is demanded, but not pruriency any more than prudery. Alas, that the paw of the modern Moloch draws into the fire so many thousands of young men and women from the homes of our land. The best capital of America is the children, and we lose too much of it in the worst of gambles—the traffic in souls.[7]

7. "Firstfruits of his creatures" (1:18). Compare 1 Corinthians 15:20, 23 for references to Christ as firstfruits. On James 1:18, one view is that James's readers were called firstfruits because they were a guarantee of many more converts to come.[8] Another view is that Christians, like the firstfruits of the Old Testament offerings of cattle, fruits and grain, should be *consecrated* to God.[9]

IV. FURTHER ADVANCED STUDY

Subjects suggested for further study are these:
1. The various dispersions of the jews, up to the present day
2. Word studies: Lord, wisdom, patience (endurance, long-suffering)
For word studies, the best outside helps are an exhaustive concordance[10] and a book on Bible words.[11]

V. APPLICATIONS

1. What have you learned from this passage, applicable to today, about
   a. prayer
   b. trial
   c. lust
   d. service to God

---

7. A.T. Robertson, *Studies in the Epistle of James*, p. 53.
8. E.g., Walter W. Wessel, "The Epistle of James," in *The Wycliffe Bible Commentary*, p. 1432.
9. See Vincent, p. 732.
10. Recommended concordances are James Strong's *Exhaustive Concordance* and Robert Young's *Analytical Concordance*.
11. Excellent word studies in the New Testament are W.E. Vine, *An Expository Dictionary of New Testament Words*, and Marvin R. Vincent, *Word Studies in the New Testament*.

    e. bright outlook on life
    f. values
    g. the heart of God
    h. responsibilities that go along with life itself
2. Why is prayer basic to Christian living?
3. Are you proud to be a bondslave of God and of the Lord Jesus Christ?

VI. WORDS TO PONDER

When all kinds of trials and temptations crowd into your lives, my brothers, don't resent them as intruders, but welcome them as friends! Realize that they come to test your faith and to produce in you the quality of endurance (1:1-3, Phillips).

Lesson 4

Doers of the Word

James has magnified God's help to his people in trials and temptations and has spoken of good gifts from above. We saw in our last lesson many such gifts, as cited in the passage. There were also exhortations and commands in the text, such as "ask in faith," but mainly James was emphasizing *God's part* in the life of the believer.

Now, beginning with the passage of this lesson, the focus turns more directly on *man's part* in this important matter of Christian living. And James knows where to begin his discussion—on the subject of the Word of God. Acceptable *works* (Christian living) must proceed from the revealed *Word* (divine standard).[1] This is reflected in Chart K, which identifies the section 1:19–2:13 as "Word and Works."

EXCERPT FROM CHART G
JAMES 1:19—4:12   **Chart K**

1:19	2:1	2:14	3:1	3:13 4:12
WORD AND WORKS		FAITH AND WORKS	TONGUE	WARS
FULFILLMENT	FAVORITISM	FALLACY	FOUNTAIN	FIGHTINGS
FAITH AT WORK (outer and inner life)				

---

1. Truly, daily *living* for the Christian must be by the same Word that originally brought new *life* to him.

47

Two segments compose the section "Word and Works." These are "Fulfillment" (having to do with *doing* the Word); and "Favoritism" (having to do with one particular violation of the Word). The study of this lesson is about the former of these, hence the title "Doers of the Word."

I. PREPARATION FOR STUDY

1. Read 1:18 again, and note how this verse, with its reference to "word of truth," is an introduction to the theme of the present passage. Observe the whole scope of salvation in this verse:

Sovereign predestination—"of his own will"
Supernatural regeneration—"begat he us"
Efficacious instrument—"with the word of truth"
Divine life and living—"firstfruits of his creatures"

2. A key phrase in this passage is "righteousness of God." James's emphasis on works is not intended to suggest that a man can attain God's righteousness by works. Read Romans 1:17, 3:21-31 for its teaching about the righteousness of God. (Note the many occurrences of the phrase "righteousness of God." Associate with this the literal meaning of the word "justified," which is "declared righteous.")

3. Always keep in mind as you study the epistle that this book was intended by God to speak to *you*.

II. ANALYSIS

Segment to be analyzed: 1:19-27
Paragraph divisions: at verses 19, 22, 26

A. General Analysis

1. Mark in your Bible the paragraph divisions shown above. Then read the segment once or twice, marking key words and phrases in your Bible as you read. What words and phrases stand out most boldly?

_____

_____

_____

2. You may want to lay out on paper a work sheet similar to the analytical Chart L. Record your various observations in the respec-

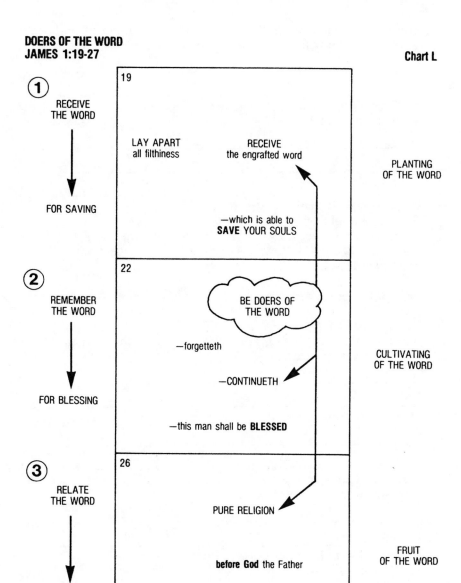

①
RECEIVE
THE WORD

↓

FOR SAVING

②
REMEMBER
THE WORD

↓

FOR BLESSING

③
RELATE
THE WORD

↓

FOR GOD

19

LAY APART
all filthiness

RECEIVE
the engrafted word

PLANTING
OF THE WORD

—which is able to
SAVE YOUR SOULS

22

BE DOERS OF
THE WORD

—forgetteth

—CONTINUETH

CULTIVATING
OF THE WORD

—this man shall be **BLESSED**

26

PURE RELIGION

before God the Father

FRUIT
OF THE WORD

—VISIT . . .
—KEEP HIMSELF . . .

27

49

tive paragraphs, and use the margins for such things as outlines.
3. In your own words, what is the main theme of this segment?

_____

4. What different aspect of that theme is taught by each of the three paragraphs?

_____

_____

5. Observe this main topical study on Chart L:
Title: Doers of the Word
Points: (1) Receive the Word, (2) Remember the Word, (3) Relate the Word. We will follow this outline in the suggestions for paragraph study below.

B. Paragraph Analysis

1. *Paragraph 1:19-21: Receive the Word*
What words of this paragraph have to do with the Christian's attitude of *receiving*, or taking in?

_____

Why is such an attitude necessary?

_____

What is meant by the word "meekness"? In answering this, consider Jesus' words of Matthew 11:29.

_____

How are the following phrases related to each other:
        "swift to hear"
        "slow to speak"
        "slow to wrath"
What is meant by verse 20? Compare a modern version's reading here.

_____

_____

50

"Superfluity of naughtiness" is better translated as "abundance of malice." What are the two contrasting commands of verse 21?

_____

_____

In what sense is the implanted ("engrafted") Word of God able to save people's souls? Compare Romans 1:16.

_____

Since James is talking to believers in this epistle, what may he have in mind when he writes, "Which is able to save your souls"? In answering this, keep in mind that the phrase preceding this is a command to Christians already saved, "Receive with meekness the engrafted word."

_____

2. *Paragraph 1:22-25: Remember the Word*
The paragraph opens with the clear command, "Be ye doers of the word, and not hearers only" (1:22; cf. Rom. 2:13). This could be called a key verse for the epistle. How does James develop this theme in the paragraph?

_____

The word that is a clue to the distinctive contribution of this paragraph to the segment is the word "forgetteth" (also "forgetful"). Which one of the following three contrasts is James making in this paragraph (examine the text carefully before answering):
    a. one who hears the Word; and one who does not hear
    b. one who hears intently; and one who does not hear intently
    c. one who hears (intently or not) but forgets and so is not a doer; and one who hears intently and becomes a doer.
Note from the illustration of verse 24 that a man can hear or study the Word attentively (which is the strength of the word translated "beholdeth") and yet forget, that is, let the Word drop there, without putting it into action. What would cause a person to be guilty of this?

_____

_____

_____

What is meant by the phrase "perfect law of liberty" (v. 25)?

_____

_____

Can you reconcile the two opposite terms "law" and "liberty"?

_____

_____

Write a list of the various truths taught by verse 25.

_____

_____

_____

_____

3. Paragraph 1:26-27: Relate the Word
In using the rare New Testament word "religious" (also "religion"), James is relating worship to behavior.[2] The contrast is between vain religion and pure religion.[3] What two examples of vain religion are cited in verse 26?

_____

_____

What two examples of pure religion are cited in verse 27?

_____

_____

Is verse 27 a *definition* of pure religion? If not, what is the verse's intention?

_____

_____

2. Read Acts 26:5 and Col. 2:18, where the same word "religion" appears, in the context of worship.
3. A broad definition of religion might be: "Religion is a man's way of life based on his beliefs."

What two important areas of Christian living are represented by the two examples of verse 27?

_____

_____

_____

III. NOTES

1. "Wherefore" (1:19). The accurate rendering should be "know ye" or "ye know." The *Berkeley* version reads, "Get this, my dear brothers."
2. "Beholding his natural face in a glass" (1:23). The word "beholding" is a strong word, meaning *attentively considering*. "It is not mere careless hearing of the word which James rebukes, but the neglect to carry into practice what is heard. One may be an attentive and critical hearer of the word, yet not a doer."[4]

The phrase "his natural face" means literally "the countenance of his birth." Apply this to the Word's ministry of showing man who he *really* is.

3. "Law of liberty" (1:25). How liberty is associated with God's law is interpreted thus by *The Wycliffe Bible Commentary:*

> Law of liberty probably means that it is a law that applies to those who have the status of freedom, not from law, but from sin and self, through the word of truth. The man who looks into this law and makes a habit of doing so . . . will become a doer of the word and find true happiness.[5]

4. "Doer of the work" (1:25). The article is absent. The intended statement is "doer of work," or, as the *Berkeley* version translates, "active worker."
5. "God and the Father" (1:27). This is correctly translated as "God and Father" or "God the Father."

IV. FURTHER ADVANCED STUDY

Subjects recommended for extended study are: (1) the place of the law of God in the life of the Christian; (2) the doctrine of Christian liberty as taught in Galatians; and (3) the responsibility of Christians to the temporal as well as spiritual needs of society.

4. Marvin R. Vincent, *Word Studies in the New Testament*, 1: 734.
5. Walter W. Wessel, "The Epistle of James," in *The Wycliffe Bible Commentary*, p. 1432.

V. APPLICATIONS

1. Try to think of different circumstances in the home and in a church fellowship where each of the exhortations "swift to hear, slow to speak, slow to wrath" is pertinent.

2. Why should a man's wrath (even that of a Christian) not compete with God's wrath?

_____

_____

3. How can God's Word do a daily *saving* work in the heart of a believer?

_____

_____

4. What causes a Christian, who reads carefully what the Bible says about a certain practice, to turn around and disobey that Word?

_____

_____

_____

5. Verse 27 speaks about a Christian's *involvement* with others and his *separation* from others. Apply this latter to the contemporary scene. How are some ways by which a Christian can defile himself with things of the world?

_____

_____

_____

VI. WORDS TO PONDER

So clear away all the foul rank growth of malice, and make a soil of humble modesty for the Word which roots itself inwardly with power to save your souls (1:21, Moffatt).

The Case Against Discrimination

The passage of this lesson applies the general teaching, be doers of the Word, to one particular situation. That situation was the problem of Christians showing partiality by favoring the rich and despising the poor.

In any free society, diversity of material wealth is inevitable. This is due to various causes, such as differences in the desire and ability to work, the wisdom in investing, and the discipline of spending. The Bible condemns neither poverty nor wealth per se. It has much to say about poor people and rich people (e.g., James 1:9-11). Among those who seek God are the rich (e.g., the rich young ruler, Luke 18:18-30) as well as the poor.

In the passage of this lesson, James is not writing about what poor or rich people should do, but about a Christian's relationship to these groups. Our task in this study is to derive the timeless, universal principles taught by James's illustration of his day, so that we can apply those principles to various similar situations confronting Christians today.

I. PREPARATION FOR STUDY

1. Think about ways in which Christians today may be guilty, knowingly or not, of showing partiality to others.

2. From your acquaintance with the gospels, what relationship did Jesus maintain with people, regardless of their position, wealth, experience, knowledge, faith, and attitude toward Him?

II. ANALYSIS

Segment to be analyzed: 2:1-13
Paragraph divisions: at verses 1, 5, 8

A. General Analysis

First read the segment for overall impressions. Then read it again, looking for one main line of thought: reasons that a Christian should not show partiality in situations similar to that of 2:2-4. Record those reasons. Compare them with the reasons shown below.

The Case Against Discrimination by Christians

1. It is not consistent with the Christian's faith and Christ's glory (2:1).
2. It is based on evil motives (2:4).
3. It is not the way of God (2:5).
4. It ignores heart attitudes in favor of external things (2:6-7).
5. It transgresses the law of love (2:8-11).
6. It disregards the surety of judgment (2:12-13).

Let us study each of these points in the context of the paragraph where each appears.

B. Paragraph Analysis

1. *Paragraph 2:1-4*
Observe which verses record James's illustration. In the illustration, what is the occasion for the believer's coming into contact with a rich man and a poor man?

___

Read the phrase of verse 1, "faith of our Lord Jesus Christ," as an objective genitive, thus: "faith in our Lord Jesus Christ." (Cf. Mark 11:22; Acts 3:16.) Whose faith and whose glory are referred to in the verse?

___

How do these suggest an answer to the original question about discrimination?

___

Is the example of Jesus indirectly suggested by any phrase of verse 1?

___

Read verse 4 in various versions. Compare this reading: "Then you are guilty of creating distinctions among yourselves and making

56

judgments based on evil motives" (*Today's English Version*). The key phrase here is "evil motives" (KJV, "evil thoughts"). What is the motive behind the favor shown the rich man?

_____

_____

2. *Paragraph 2:5-7*
What example of God's ways is cited here?

_____

_____

Verse 5 is a good example of the complete circle of activity in salvation from divine sovereignty ("chosen") to man's free will ("love him"). Observe the parts of this verse in this diagram:

ACTIVITY IN SALVATION　　　　　　　　　　　　　　　　**Chart M**
JAMES 2:5

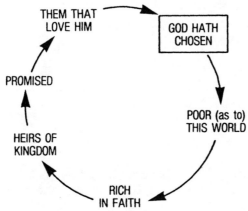

On God's outreach to poor people, read Luke 4:18 (Is. 60:1 ff); Luke 7:22; 1 Corinthians 1:27-31.
What point is made by verses 6-7?

_____

_____

Who is the one referred to in the phrase "worthy name by the which ye are called" (2:7)?

_____

_____

What is the degree of this sin: "blaspheme that worthy name"?

_____

_____

3. *Paragraph 2:8-13*
What arguments against showing partiality appear in this paragraph?

_____

_____

_____

Does James clearly identify discrimination as *sin?*

_____

_____

What is James's purpose in verses 10-11?

_____

_____

What is the point of verses 12-13?

_____

_____

In connection with future judgment for all believers, read Romans 14:10 and 2 Corinthians 5:10.

III. NOTES

1. "Assembly" (2:2). This translates the Greek word for "synagogue." In these early days of the church, the words "synagogue" and "church" (*ekklesia*, as in 5:14) were sued synonymously. On the word "synagogue" (KJV, "assembly") as used in 2:2, Vincent writes,

> The simplest explanation appears to be that the word designates the place of meeting for the Christian body, James using the word most familiar to the Jewish Christians . . . . From Acts vi. 9, we learn that there were numerous synagogues in Jerusalem, representing different bodies, such as the descendants of Jewish freedmen at Rome, and the Alexandrian or Hellenistic Jews. Among these would be the synagogue of the Christians, and such would be the case in all large cities where the dispersed Jews congregated.[1]

1. Marvin R. Vincent, *Word Studies in the New Testament*, 1: 737.

2. "Judges of [with] evil thoughts" (2:4). *The Wycliffe Bible Commentary* rightly calls these "false-value judges."[2]

3. "The poor of this world [to be] rich in faith" (2:5). The phrase should be read with the parenthetical thought understood.

4. "Worthy name by the which ye are called" (2:7). This is a reference to Christ, amplifying the Christological content of the epistle.

5. "The royal law" (2:8). Vincent says this law of love is called "the royal law" because it is "the king of all laws."[3] (Cf. Rom. 13:10; Gal. 5:14.) Another intent of this term is suggested by Williams' New Testament translation: "But if you really observe the law of the King."

6. "Convinced" (2:9). This King James English word is the equivalent of our "convicted."

7. "Mercy rejoiceth against judgment" (2:13). The *Berkeley* version reads, "Mercy triumphs over judgment."

IV. FURTHER ADVANCED STUDY

1. Study the attribute of *glory* as it is related to Jesus Christ (2:1). Key passages include John 1:14; 2 Corinthians 4:6; Hebrews 1:3; 1 Corinthians 2:8; Acts 7:2; Ephesians 1:17.

2. The reference to "assembly" ("synagogue") in 2:2 suggests a subject for extended study. With the help of outside sources such as a Bible encyclopedia, compare a Jewish synagogue service of Jesus' day and a Christian local church service at the end of the first century. What kind of a worship service do you think the Jewish Christians of James's epistle participated in?

V. APPLICATIONS

1. Have you ever been guilty of showing partiality to one group as over against another, with wrong motives?

2. Do you think more poor people would attend church if they knew they would not be looked down upon by some of the church's members?

3. What are your thoughts about riches and poverty? Is a person's character affected by either of these? Is it true that extreme poverty may be a peril to a man's soul, as great wealth may be?

4. What does it really mean to "love thy neighbour as thyself" (2:8)?

2. Walter W. Wessel, "The Epistle of James" in *The Wycliffe Bible Commentary*, p. 1433.
3. Vincent, p. 741.

59

5. Apply this quote to the contemporary scene: "A person needs full knowledge of the social conditions about him and the courage to apply the gospel of Christ to these conditions. But let no one imagine that sociology can take the place of the gospel of Jesus. Christianity is sociological, but sociology is not necessarily Christian."[4]

VI. WORDS TO PONDER

My brothers, stop trying to maintain your faith in our Lord Jesus Christ, the glorious presence of God on earth, along with acts of partiality to certain ones (2:1, Williams).

---

4. A.T. Robertson, *Studies in the Epistle of James*, p. 85.

Lesson 6

James 2:14-26

The Faith That Saves

When James wrote this epistle, Christianity was still something very new, uniquely so for believers. They were on the inside, and it was a new *experience.* But to those on the outside—the unbeliever—it was a new *religion.*

James knew that faith was the basic ingredient of the new experience. In fact, before he was saved, his real problem was that he could not *believe* that Jesus was the Christ. His burden in writing the epistle was to show his Christian brethren that the faith that saves can be the only *genuine* faith. And if it is genuine, it is real, alive, of the heart, dynamic, productive, and seen of men by way of action. James knew that if the local Christian group could be instructed and encouraged about what saving faith really was, then the world outside—looking in, as it were—would discover that Christianity was not another cult or religion, but a new life from above.

I. PREPARATION FOR STUDY

1. Read Romans 3:21–5:2 for Paul's teaching about justification by faith. Paul says a person is not justified by works (e.g., Rom. 4:2, 6); whereas in the present passage of James we learn that Abraham was justified by works (James 2:21). contradictory as the two passages may appear, there really is no problem when one considers the fact that Paul only denies works as the root of salvation.[1] Paul is not writing about Christian conduct as such but about the way to becoming a Christian. James is not denying faith as the way of salvation, but he is maintaining that works will issue from a faith that is genuine. D. A. Hayes writes:

1. Read such passages as Titus 1:16; 3:8; 1 Tim. 6:18, which show the important place Paul assigns to works as the outcome of salvation.

Paul is looking at the root; James is looking at the fruit. Paul is talking about the beginning of the Christian life; James is talking about its continuance and consummation. With Paul, the works he renounces are dead works. With James, the faith he denounces is apart from works and is a dead faith.[2]

Your analysis of the passage of this lesson will focus on how James identifies genuine faith, or "The Faith That Saves."

2. James refers to three Old Testament stories from which he derives teachings about faith and works. Read each story, and answer the questions below.

a. Genesis 15:1-6. Why was Abraham declared righteous? (Note: Justification is the sovereign act of God in declaring a man positionally righteous.)

_____

_____

b. Genesis 22:1-19. What was Abraham really commended for on this occasion: (1) placing his son on the altar (22:9-10); (2) a fear of God (22:12) and faith in Him (22:8); or (3) both? Compare Hebrews 11:17-19, which is a New Testament commentary on this. Note how the Hebrews writer relates the Genesis 22 story to the Genesis 15 story.

c. Joshua 2:1-21 (cf. Heb. 11:31). What did Rahab *do* to bring about her physical safety?

_____

_____

Why did she believe?

_____

_____

Read Joshua 6:25 and Matthew 1:5 to learn something of her life after this event.

3. Read 1:19-27 to review what James had written earlier about *works* (e.g., "Be ye doers of the word").

4. The punctuation of verse 18 is difficult to determine.[3] Two views held about this are:

   a. All the words of verse 18 from "Thou hast" to "my works" are spoken words of the man.[4]

2. D.A. Hayes, "The Epistle of James," in *The International Standard Bible Encyclopedia,* 3: 1566.

3. The original manuscripts and the earliest copies did not contain punctuation marks.

4. See *The Living New Testament* (Wheaton, Ill.: Tyndale, 1967) and Andrew McNab, "The General Epistle of James," in *The New Bible Commentary,* p. 112.

b. Just the first statement represents the spoken words of the man: "Thou has faith, and I have works."[5] The remainder of the verse quotes James. The position taken in this manual reconstructs the verse in this manner (see Chart N):

> Yea, a man may say [to you] "Thou hast faith [only], and I have works [only]." [But I say to you], "Show me thy faith without thy works [which you really cannot do], and I will show thee my faith by my works."

Keep this paraphrase in mind as you study this lesson.

II. ANALYSIS

Segment to be analyzed: 2:14-26
Paragraph divisions: at verses 14, 18, 19, 21, 25

A. General Analysis

Mark paragraph divisions in your Bible at the verses noted above.[6]
Read the entire segment and observe how a statement relating faith and works appears at the end of each of the paragraphs. Read the passage again. What is James's main point here?

_____

_____

Read the paragraphs one by one. Record a main theme for each:
2:14-17

_____

2:18

_____

2:19-20

_____

2:21-24

_____

2:25-26

_____

5. See *The New Berkeley Version in Modern English* (Grand Rapids: Zondervan, 1969), N.T., p. 254, and Walter W. Wessel, "The Epistle of James," in *The Wycliffe Bible Commentary*, p. 1434.
6. This segment could be divided into paragraphs at other points.

An outline for this segment is difficult to detect. Chart N is given in detail here as an aid to seeing something of the flow of James's message. Study the chart carefully, and observe the following:

1. The title of the segment is "The Faith That Saves." What verse in the segment contains the word "save"?

2. Observe that the segment is divided into two main parts, each of which is of two parts:

> THE FAITH THAT SAVES
> It is a Faith That Produces Works (2:14-18).
> Works are faith's partner (2:14-17).
> Works are faith's demonstrators (2:18).
> A Faith That Comes from the Heart (2:19-26)
> It is not mere intellectual assent (2:19-20).
> It is heart obedience (2:21-26).

Study carefully the text of the segment to see how this outline was derived. You may want to revise the outline in some places.

3. Observe the many places where the phrase (or its equivalent) "faith without works is dead" appears.

Now that we have studied the segment as a whole, let us examine each paragraph in more detail.

B. Paragraph Analysis

1. *Paragraph 2:14-17: Works are faith's partner.*
The last two words of the paragraph are the clue to the main point made here. what are they?

_____

_____

The sense of the phrase "can faith save him?" of verse 14 is this: "Can [such a] faith save him?"[7] James does not deny the efficacy of genuine faith (cf. 2:23; also 2:5).
What is he emphasizing?

_____

_____

---

7. The article "the" modifies "faith" in the original, and has the force of "that" (or "such a") in the context.

THE FAITH THAT SAVES
JAMES 2:14-26

IS A FAITH THAT PRODUCES WORKS ①

WORKS ARE FAITH'S PARTNER	WORKS ARE FAITH'S DEMONSTRATORS
14	18
What profit? —though a man	yea, a man may say (to you)
SAY HE HATH FAITH, AND HAVE NOT WORKS.	(But I say to you)
CAN (SUCH A) FAITH SAVE HIM?	**Show me** THY FAITH without thy works
(illustration)	I will **show thee** MY FAITH by my works.
What profit?	
Even so,	
FAITH, if it hath not works,	
IS DEAD, being **ALONE.**	
17	

② IS A FAITH THAT COMES FROM THE HEART	Chart N

NOT MERE INTELLECTUAL ASSENT

19
Thou believest . . . .
The devils also believe . . . . .
But wilt thou know . . . . .
FAITH WITHOUT WORKS IS DEAD?

BUT HEART OBEDIENCE

illustration . . 1	illustration . . 2
21	25
ABRAHAM —justified by works	RAHAB —justified by works
By WORKS a man is JUSTIFIED, and NOT BY FAITH ONLY	SO FAITH WITHOUT WORKS IS DEAD ALSO.
24	26

65

Why do you think he uses such strong terminology?

_____

_____

What is the main point of the illustration of verses 15 and 16?

_____

_____

How does it support James's point?

_____

_____

(Observe the common word "profit" in vv. 14 and 16.) The core of verse 17 is "Faith ... is Dead." What really is meant by this strong descriptive word "dead"?

_____

_____

2. *Paragraph 2:18: Works are faith's demonstrators.* (Refer back to the earlier part of this lesson where the punctuation of this verse was discussed.)

The clue words of this paragraph's main point are "show me." Observe how the "man" of v. 18a disagrees with what James had just established, that works are faith's *partners.* The man says, in effect,

"Thou hast faith [only]"
"I have works [only]"

What is the plain fallacy in such a position?

_____

_____

James now tests the man's claim by using the measuring stick of *demonstration* . Can one person "see" another person's faith without the presence of works? Can one person "see" another person's faith by observing his works? James of course is not dealing here with the possibility of hypocrisy, where external works falsely represent the internal. He is talking about *genuine* works in connection with *genuine* faith.

3. *Paragraph 2:19-20. Saving faith is not mere intellectual assent.* According to verse 20, what kind of man is James addressing in these verses?

_____

_____

Is this one of James's Christian brethren? Read verse 14 again and note that James distinguishes between his brethren and the unsaved 'man.'" This is the same group represented by the "man" of verse 18. Now, in verse 19, the same group of unbelievers is addressed by the word "Thou."

What kind of believing is illustrated by verse 19?

_____

_____

What does this teach about what saving faith is?

_____

_____

How does verse 20, with its familiar phrase about faith and works, support the truth taught in verse 19?

_____

_____

Do demons produce works?[8] If so, what kind?

_____

_____

4. *Paragraph 2:21-24.Saving faith is heart obedience—Illustration 1.* 1.
Who are the two persons used as illustrations in 2:21-26? Compare "our father" (v. 21) and "the harlot" (v. 25).

_____

_____

Review the study you made earlier in the lesson about Abraham in Genesis 15 and 22.

Observe the two appearances of the word "justified" in this paragraph. The root of this word in the Greek is "righteous," so that to be justified is to be declared righteous. Some interpret the word in these two places as meaning "justified before men" (contrasting it with Paul's emphasis in Romans on being "justified before God"). The other view is that, on the basis of verse 24, James

8. The Greek should be translated "demons," and "devils," as the KJV has it.

must be thinking about justification before God, by bringing in the phrase "not by faith only" (only God can actually *see* our faith). How is this view supported by the phrase of verse 23, "imputed [reckoned] unto him for righteousness"?

_____

_____

Study verse 23 in connection with Genesis 15:1-6. Was Abraham's faith of the heart?

_____

_____

Study verses 21-22 in connection with Genesis 22:1-19. Was Abraham's obedience of the heart?

_____

_____

How are the following related to each other (listed here in no particular order):
FAITH—WORKS—HEART—OBEDIENCE—MIND

_____

_____

_____

5. *Paragraph 2:25-26: Saving faith is heart obedience—Illustration 2.*
Review the study you made earlier in the lesson about Rahab in Joshua 2:1-21.
Read Hebrews 11:31 again, and note the words "faith" and "believed" in that short commentary on Rahab. What indications are there in the Joshua account that Rahab came to the place of *belief?*

_____

_____

_____

Hebrews 11:31 makes reference to the *physical* deliverance of Rahab ("perished not"). From the Joshua passage (2:1-21) and from Joshua 6:25 and Matthew 1:5 we learn that Rahab's deliverance was more than physical.

By saying "likewise also" (2:25) James is telling us that the illustration of Rahab teaches the same truth as the illustration of Abraham. What is it?

_____

_____

What does the illustration of 2:26*a* teach about the relation between faith and works?

_____

_____

Make a summary of the segment 2:14-26 by listing the various truths it teaches concerning faith, works and salvation.

III. NOTES

1. "The devils [demons] also believe, and tremble" (2:19). The word "tremble" appears only here in the New Testament. The word meant originally "to be rough on the surface; to bristle." There is the suggestion of "a horror which makes the hair stand on end and contracts the surface of the skin, making 'gooseflesh.'"[9] Why is a serious contemplation of the existence of a supreme God such an awesome experience?

2. 'O vain man" (2:20). The word for "vain" is better translated "empty," which in this context would mean without spiritual life.

3. "Abraham our father" (2:21). Read Galatians 3:6-29 for the teaching that Abraham is the spiritual father of all true believers.

4. "By works was faith made perfect" (2:22). The word translated "perfect" has the idea of fulfillment, or reaching a goal. The *Berkeley* version reads verse 22 thus: "You see how his faith cooperated with his works and how faith *reached its supreme expression* through his works."

5. "Friend of God" (2:23). Read 2 Chronicles 20:7 and Isaiah 41:8 for references to Abraham as "friend" of God. Actually, the Hebrew in both verses is literally translated as "beloved." The "friend of God" is still the favorite title of Abraham among Jews and Muhammadans.

6. "Rahab the harlot" (2:25). There were many illustrations that James could have drawn upon to supplement that of Abraham, but he chose the story of a Gentile harlot to demonstrate the universal application of the truth he was teaching.

9. Marvin R. Vincent, *Word Studies in the New Testament*, 1: 744.

From the story of Rahab many lessons may be learned, two of which are cited here:[10]

a. *God saves, not because of one's righteousness, but because of one's faith.*

Rahab was a prostitute, an unbelieving Gentile. So God's saving her was not because she was good, but that she might become so.

It is not to be supposed from Hebrews 11:31 and James 2:25 that God commended Rahab's falsehood or any of her other sins. These passages point out her living faith, which was manifested by her works that followed.

In the same way the thief on the cross was saved by faith. He abundantly proved the reality of his faith by his works that followed, namely: confession of his own guilt, public confession of faith in Christ's power to save, his fear of God, his rebuking of sin, his calling upon Christ to remember him—all seen in his few words as he hung on the cross (see Luke 23:39-43).

b. *God has rich rewards for those who believe and obey Him.*

Joshua 6:25 and Matthew 1:5 tell how Rahab's ensuing years were blessed of God. When her life was spared she joined the people of God and dwelt among them. Later on she married one of the men of Judah, Salmon (thought by some to be one of the spies whose life she saved), and became one of the ancestors of the Lord Jesus Christ.

How exceeding abundantly God wrought for her above all that she asked or thought! He saved her from death, placed her among His children, enlightened and instructed her, brought her into the royal line, and gave her a part in Christ.

On the story of Rahab, A.T. Robertson writes:

> It was a crisis in the history of Israel as they came to Jericho, and Rahab took her stand for God at the start; hence the high honor accorded her.... Certainly there is no desire in James nor in Hebrews to dignify her infamous trade, which she renounced, but only to single her out as a brand snatched from the burning by the power of God.[11]

---

10. See Irving L. Jensen, *Joshua,* Self-Study Guide (Chicago: Moody, 1968), pp. 19-20.
11. A.T. Robertson, *Studies in the Epistle of James,* p. 102.

IV. FURTHER ADVANCED STUDY

Subjects recommended for extended study are:
1. New Testament teaching on justification; faith
2. Paul's teaching on works
3. various views of commentaries and Bible versions on the punctuation of verse 18

V. APPLICATIONS

Name any five basic doctrines of the Christian faith, and show how such a faith must inevitably produce good works. (For example, a Christian who believes that salvation is by God's grace will show kindness even to mean people whom he contacts in everyday living.)

VI. WORDS TO PONDER

Can't you see that his [Abraham's] faith and his actions were, so to speak, partners—that his faith was implemented by his deed? (2:22, Phillips).

Lesson 7

The Christian and His Tongue

James now applies the basic truth of 2:14-26, that faith without works is dead, to everyday Christian living. The two areas of application are speech (subject of this lesson) and strife (subject to the next lesson). Observe on Chart O how the passage of this lesson (3:1-12) relates to its surroundings. Study the chart also as a way to review the material studied in the previous lessons. Observe James's pattern: establishing first the basic truths (principles involved); then applying them to everyday life (examples). (Cf. Chart O with survey Chart G.)

FAITH WITHOUT WORKS
JAMES 1:19—4:12

Chart O

1:19	2:1	2:14	3:1	3:13 4:12
Lesson 4	Lesson 5	Lesson 6	Lesson 7	Lesson 8
WORD AND WORKS		FAITH AND WORKS		
principle discussed	an example	principle discussed	example of tongue	example of strife
FULFILLMENT	FAVORITISM	FALLACY	FOUNTAIN	FIGHTINGS

I. PREPARATION FOR STUDY

1. First read the passage in a modern paraphrase, to catch the main flow of the segment. Try to visualize the setting of this por-

72

tion of James's epistle. James makes some strong statements about the tongue. What situations may have developed in the lives of these Jewish Christians that caused James to make such a big issue of this problem? Think of similar circumstances in which Christians today commit the same kinds of sin.

_____

_____

2. Reflect on what is involved in these three activities: thought; word; action. Think about motives; ones affected; possibility of misunderstanding; repentance and recovery. If deeds ("be doers of the word") are crucial in effective Christian living, are spoken words any less crucial? Explain.

_____

_____

3. Read these other verses in James about speech: 1:19, 26; 4:11, 12; 5:12.

II. ANALYSIS

Segment to be analyzed: 3:1-12
Paragraph divisions: at verses 1, 3, 5b, 7, 9

A. General Analysis

1. After you have marked the paragraph divisions in your Bible, read the segment to determine the main point of each paragraph. (For the first paragraph, read the word "masters" as "teachers," in v. 1. See Notes.) Record the theme of each paragraph below:
3:1-2

_____

3-5a

_____

5b-6

_____

7-8

_____

9-12

_____

2. James's illustrations are drawn mainly from what sources?

_____

_____

Compare this type with that of Jesus. Compare it also with that of
Paul. What teaching methods can be learned from James's use of
illustrations?

_____

_____

3. Is James writing here about the tongue of a believer or unbeliever?

_____

_____

Observe the occurrences of the phrase "my brethren."
4. All five paragraphs have something to say about the spoken
word. The first paragraph *introduces* the subject. How accurate
would it be to say that the remaining four paragraphs give *descriptions* of the tongue? Try to arrive at an outline for these four paragraphs, as to how the tongue is described.

_____

_____

_____

B. Paragraph Analysis

1. *Paragraph 3:1-2: The subject of the tongue introduced.*
The opening command, "Be not many masters [teachers],"
has been interpreted in at least two different ways. One view sees
the teachers as judges of other people's lives; the other view is
that the teachers are instructors of the truth in the community of
believers. Let us look into both of these views, in the light of the
remainder of the paragraph.

a. Teachers are judges of other people's lives. Read Romans
2:21, and observe how the word "teachest" is used here. (This is
the same Greek root translated "master" in James 3:1, AV.) Compare Romans 2:1 and observe how the word "teachest" is used
here. (This is the same Greek root translated "master" in James
3:1, KJV.) Compare Romans 2:1, where Paul uses the stronger
word "judgest," with a similar intent. (Note in this verse also that
Paul brings in the thought of condemnation: "Thou condemnest
thyself.")

74

Now read James 3:1 again, and see how the verse could be taken to refer to teachers who judge others but refuse to judge themselves. On this John Calvin writes:

> I take masters not to be those who performed a public duty in the Church, but such as took upon them the right of passing judgment upon others: for such reprovers sought to be accounted as masters of morals.[1]

This also is the interpretation presented by the *Living Bible*'s paraphrase of 3:1-2*a*: "Dear brothers, don't be too eager to tell others their faults, for we all make many mistakes."[2] If this was James's intention, it also clearly explains the first sentence of verse 2, "For in many things we all stumble." (The word "stumble" is a better translation than "offend" of KJV.)

The one question still raised by this view, however, is why James would say, "Be not many judges" rather than "be not judges at all." One answer to this is that while James recognized that some Christians are divinely called to the task of admonishing the brethren, he was thinking of the other kind—the large group —who had "that immoderate desire to condemn, which proceeds from ambition and pride, when any one exalts himself against his neighbors."[3] Hence James was saying, in effect, "Be not among those many censorious judges."

b. Teachers as instructors of other Christians. This is the view held by most Bible expositors and translators. Read 3:1-2 in various versions to confirm this. A study of the word *teacher* (Greek, *didaskaloi*) in a concordance will show that the word is practically always used in the sense of instruction—formal or informal. The questions given below are geared to this view of the phrase of 3:1, "Be not many teachers."

Do you think James had in mind here Christian brethren who had received a divine call to teach? (On the gift of teaching, read Rom. 12:6-8; 1 Cor. 12:27-31; Eph. 4:11.) Or do you think he is re-

---

1. John Calvin, *Commentaries on the Catholic Epistles* (Edinburgh: Calvin Trans. Soc., 1855), pp. 317-18. Read G. Coleman Luck, *James, Faith in Action,* pp. 64-66, for a presentation of this view.
2. A Bible paraphrase such as *The Living Bible* is not strictly a translation, and so the author(s) can take the liberty of incorporating an interpretation in the Bible text.
3. Calvin, p. 318.

ferring more to teachers among the laity, such as the kind referred to in 1 Timothy 1:6-7?

_____

_____

What really is James cautioning about when he says that not many of his readers should strive to be teachers?

_____

_____

Read 1 Corinthians 4:14-17, and observe why Paul was such an effective teacher. What reason does James give for a person to think twice before becoming a teacher? (3:1b)

_____

_____

What principle of accountability is involved here?

_____

_____

Verse 2 is divided into two sentences. What key word is common to both?

_____

_____

What fact is stated in the first sentence?

_____

_____

What kind of person is described in the second sentence?

_____

_____

Is the reference to "word" intended to mean the spoken word?

_____

_____

Who is a "perfect man" such as James describes in verse 2? Recall your study of the word "perfect" in 1:4.

_____

How does James relate the tongue to the whole body? Illustrate this truth by examples from everyday living.

_____

Now that you have studied 3:1-2 from two differing interpretations of the word translated "master," what view do you favor?

2. *Paragraph 3:3-5a: The influential tongue.*

What two illustrations are given here? What are the common elements of each illustration?

_____

Verse 5a with its connective "even so" tells us the main point of the illustrations of horses and ships. What is that main point?

_____

In what ways can a person influence others by the spoken word?

_____

List some examples of constructive and destructive influence:

CONSTRUCTIVE	DESTRUCTIVE
Words of encouragement	Discouragement
Gentleness	Anger
Kindness	Hate
Patience	Rude joking
Love	Name calling

Can you think of an occasion when the delivery of cold words of truth could have a destructive effect on the life of a person hearing them? Justify your answer.

_____

_____

Can the spoken words of a person turn around, as it were, and influence the speaker himself in any way? Answer this after you have first reflected on the difference between thoughts kept to oneself and those same thoughts that on another occasion are spoken to someone.

Do you think the phrase "and boasteth great things" (v. 5) is a reference to evil conceit or righteous pride?

3. *Paragraph 3:5b-6: The destructive tongue.*
What is the key repeated word in this short paragraph?

_____

Are the fires of these verses the helpful kind or the harmful?
The basic metaphor of the paragraph is "the tongue is a fire" (v. 6). What different description of the tongue as fire is given by each of the following phrases:

   "How great a matter [forest] a little fire kindleth"
   "A world of iniquity"
   "Defileth the whole body" (cf. Mark 7:15, 20, 23)
   "Setteth on fire the course of nature" (Do you think the phrase "course of nature" has particular reference to a person's life or only general reference to all of God's creation.)
   "It is set on fire of [by] hell"

What is the source of evil speech?

_____

_____

What does this suggest as to the corrective for such destructive activity?

_____

_____

4. *Paragraph 3:7-8: The untameable tongue.*
What sober fact about the tongue is stated in verse 8*a*?

_____

_____

Since man has been able to tame animal life (v. 7), what does his inability to tame the tongue tell us about man himself and about speech itself?

_____

_____

"Unruly evil" (v. 8*b*) means "restless evil." Since the tongue can be such a *restless* instrument, what critical situation is suggested by the further description that it is "full of deadly poison" (v. 8*b*)? (Cf. Ps. 140:3 for its reference to poison.)

_____

_____

What kinds of speech by a person would be classified as *deadly poison*?

_____

_____

5. *Paragraph 3:9-12: The inconsistent tongue.*
Has James been writing these strong descriptions of the tongue primarily for the benefit of believers or unbelievers? (See v. 10.)

_____

_____

The last phrase of verse 10 is the first *appeal* of James concerning the tongue in this chapter since the *command* of 3:1. Would you not say, however, that the very tone of James's entire treatise is one of rebuke and warning? (For example, "The tongue is a fire, a world of iniquity.")

_____

_____

List the examples of *inconsistency* of the tongue cited by James in verses 9 and 10.

_____

_____

List the illustrations from nature that show the *consistent* functioning of the nonhuman creation of God: (Cf. Jesus' illustrations of Luke 6:43; Matt. 7:16.)

_____

_____

What does this contrast teach about man? (Compare this contrast with that about taming given in vv. 7 and 8.)

_____

_____

Why is the praise of God such a vital function and privilege for the Christian?

_____

_____

What verses or chapters from the Bible comes to mind as you think of the praise of God? (Read Ps. 146; 51:14-15; Luke 1:64-79 as examples.)
Someone has called a backbiting tongue a "third tongue," injuring three persons: the one who utters the slander, the one who listens, and the one of whom the slander is told.[4] What causes a Christian after he has spoken words of praise to God, to turn around and speak evil against a man (cf. Rom. 12:14)? What does this reveal about such a Christian's true relationship to God?

_____

_____

Why is it to important for a Christian to view every person as a creature of God, "made after the similitude of God" ("in the likeness of God")?

_____

_____

What different things are taught in this paragraph about hypocrisy?

_____

_____

Does anyone like a hypocrite?
"The crisp wisdom of James about the tongue makes one wonder afresh if his mother had not taught him some of these aphorisms as a child."[5] What do you think?

---

4. See A.T. Robertson, _Studies in the Epistle of James_, p. 123.
5. Ibid.

III. NOTES

1. "Be not many masters" (3:1). The Greek word *didaskaloi* really means "teachers" and is so translated in most versions. Moffatt translates the phrase as "Do not swell the ranks of the teachers." Here James is "warning against the too eager and general assumption of the privilege of teaching, which was not restricted to a particular class, but was exercised by believers generally."[6] The privilege of anyone speaking—thus "teaching"—in the meetings of the early groups of Jewish Christians was a carry over from the Jewish synagogue services, where even strangers were allowed to speak. Recall from the gospels how Jesus took advantage of this opportunity (Matt. 12:9 ff.; Mark 1:39; Luke 6:6 ff.). The book of Acts also reveals that the apostles used this synagogue privilege to preach the gospel (e.g., Acts 13:15 ff.). James is not restricting the privilege of teaching in the local congregations, but he is warning against the abuse of this privilege.

2. "Offend" (3:2). The Greek word means literally to "stumble," which is a better translation. *Today's English Version* translates this sentence, "All of us often make mistakes."

3. "Very small helm" (3:4). A modern application of this first-century illustration carries the same lesson. The helm of the modern transatlantic ocean liner is a complex electronic instrument, but it is still "very small" compared to the giant ship. The awesome wonder of such big things in the world is that so small an object can determine their destiny.

4. "How great a matter a little fire kindleth" (3:5). The primary meaning of the word translated "matter" is "wood" or "forest." Most versions so translate the word.

5. "Defileth the whole body" (3:6). Jesus said, "That which proceedeth out of the mouth, this defileth the man" (Matt. 15:11, ADV). A.T. Robertson makes an interesting observation concerning the defiling effect of words: "At first James seems to overstate the matter, but modern science reinforces his point. It is now known that angry words cause the glands of the body to discharge a dangerous poison that affects the stomach, the heart, the brain."[7]

6. "Course of nature" (3:6). The phrase used by James here has reference to a person's whole human existence. *The New Berkeley Version* reads "whole round of existence." Vincent translates the Greek literally as "wheel of birth," that is, the wheel that is set in motion at birth and runs on to the close of life. "This revolving wheel is kindled by the tongue, and rolls on in de-

6. Marvin R. Vincent, *Word Studies in the New Testament*, 1:746.
7. Robertson, p. 116.

structive blaze. . . . The tongue works the chief mischief, kindles the most baleful fires in the course of life."[8]

7. "It is set on fire of hell" (3:6). The Greek noun translated "hell" is *gehenna*, which is a transliteration of the Aramaic form of the Hebrew *ge-ben-hinnom* ("valley of the son of Hinnom"). The English word *Gehenna* comes from the Greek word. *The New Berkeley Version* writes of this:

> Gehenna is sometimes used to denote the Valley of Hinnom, a place where human sacrifices were once made, Jer. 7:31. In this valley refuse was burned. Consequently fires were constantly going. The Israelites used the word "Gehenna" to express the eternal judgment of the wicked. Jesus employed it here and elsewhere, e.g., Matt. 5:22, to illustrate the consequence of sin. Cf. "lake of fire," Rev. 10:20.[9]

James is saying in this verse that the destructive fire of the tongue has its source in the fires of hell. One has aptly remarked, "The fires of Pentecost will not rest where the fires of Gehenna are working."

8. "Similitude of God" (3:9). This is the "image" and "likeness" of God referred to in Genesis 1:26. It is not a physical likeness but a spiritual one, involving the whole immaterial part of man.

9. "Sweet water and bitter" (3:11); "salt water and fresh" (3:12). Water is either good ("sweet," "fresh") or bad ("bitter," "salt") for drinking. Bad water can be made good (e.g., 2 Kings 2:19-22). And good water can become bad (e.g., the bitter waters of Marah, Ex. 15:23, and the salt waters of the Dead Sea). "But water is not sweet and bitter at the same time from the same fountain. You have sweet water on Hermon and salt water in the Dead Sea . . . but not both in the same place."[10]

IV. FURTHER ADVANCED STUDY

Subjects recommended for further study are:

1. The ministry of teaching. Study what the Bible has to say about these two different teaching ministries by Christians: (a) formal teaching (e.g., a teacher-preacher, with the gift of teaching); and (b) informal teaching, the kind that all believers should engage in to some degree.

8. Vincent, 1: 749.
9. Footnote to Mark 9:43, *The New Berkeley Version in Modern English*, N.T., p. 47.
10. Robertson, p. 122.

2. The praise of God. This is an extensive subject in the Bible because the glory of God is the object of all His creation. Study especially motives, forms, and fruits of true praise of God.

3. The doctrine of hell. A theology or doctrine book will be of much help here.[11]

V. APPLICATIONS

Many applications may be made of this passage because *speaking* is such a busy activity of all people. Make a list of all the lessons taught by the passage concerning the Christian's tongue. Included in your list will no doubt be applications suggested in the following items:

1. What about judging others? Should you judge a person's motives? What should be your own motive in evaluating the actions of another person?

2. Why is the spoken word so powerful in influencing other people's lives?

3. Think of various ways that evil speech can be a destructive fire.

4. How common among Christians is the inconsistency spoken of by Jesus in Luke 6:46? How does your own life measure up to the truth Jesus is asserting here?

VI. WORDS TO PONDER

The tongue "is first inflamed by hell . . . and then inflames all the wheel of nature"—the chariot wheel of man as he advances on the way of life. "But one must not forget that while the tongue can be set on fire of hell, it can also be touched by a live coal from God's altar."[12] Isaiah said,

> Woe is me! For I am undone; because I am a man of unclean lips, and I dwell in the midst of a people of unclean lips: for mine eyes have seen the King, Jehovah of hosts. Then flew one of the seraphim unto me, having a live coal in his hand, which he had taken with the tongs from off the altar: and he touched my mouth with it, and said, Lo, this hath touched thy lips and thine iniquity is taken away, and thy sin forgiven (Isa. 6:5-7, ASV).

11. For a concise treatment of the subject of Gehenna, see *Zondervan Pictorial Bible Dictionary* (Grand Rapids: Zondervan, 1963), p. 303.
12. Ibid., p. 117.

Lesson 8

James 3:13–4:12

The Evils of Faction Among Christians

The subject of the previous lesson was the Christian and his speech; now it is the Christian and strife. When James wrote about the tongue, there was nothing mediocre in his tone. For he well knew the awesome power of the tongue. When he writes in the passage of this lesson about strife among believers, his pen is at its sharpest and boldest: "Ye lust . . . ye kill . . . ye fight and war!" (4:2). What a tragic state of affairs, James must have thought, when joint heirs of the Prince of Peace are mauling each other to grab a selfish prize.

The stage of this world of people has always been that of communal life. The family, fellowship, neighborhood, city, nation, world—all of these have existed since the dawning hours of history. There is no such thing as a real hermit. No one lives in isolation. Christians, of all people, should know their obligations to others—to their unsaved neighbors, and to their brethren in the Christian fellowship. And yet, for some reason, Christians often are prone to suspect, envy and even hate those who are their brothers and sisters in Christ. This was the condition among the group of James's readers, and it grieved him sorely. Hence this passage in his letter.

I. PREPARATION FOR STUDY

1. Review the survey Chart G to recall the context of the passage that will now be analyzed. You will see that this passage winds up the section of James's epistle which we have called "Practices for the Present" (1:19–4:12). In the segment that follows this (4:13–5:12), James writes about "Prizes (and judgments) in the Future."

2. Refer also to Chart O of the last lesson for another view of context.

84

3. Contemplate the setting that brought on this segment of James's epistle. One writer describes it this way:

> These verses reveal an appalling state of moral depravity in these *Diaspora* congregations; strife, self-indulgence, lust, murder, covetousness, adultery, envy, pride and slander are rife; the conception of the nature of prayer seems to have been altogether wrong among these people, and they appear to be given over wholly to a life of pleasure.[1]

What do you think are some of the causes of such a state of depravity? Does it surprise you that corruption set in so quickly in the experience of the early Christian church? You may want to read other parts of the New Testament that reveal similar problems in the young local congregations of other areas (e.g., Acts 4-5, 1 Corinthians, Galatians, 1 and 2 Thessalonians).

4. As you study this passage, be on the lookout especially for *solutions* to the problems James exposes.

5. Get a work sheet ready to record your studies. It is important that you write down your observations, whatever method of recording you choose to use. If you use some form of an analytical chart, draw on a work sheet a rectangle with four paragraph boxes such as appears in Chart P.

II. ANALYSIS

Segment to be analyzed: 3:13–4:12
Paragraph divisions: at 3:13; 4:1; 4, 11

A. General Analysis

1. Mark the paragraph divisions shown above in your Bible. Then read the segment the first time for first impressions. Mark words and phrases in your Bible which strike you as significant at this stage of your study.

2. Read the segment again, paragraph by paragraph, and try to determine a main theme for each paragraph. Record these:

3:13-18

_____

4:1-3

_____

1. W. Oesterley, quoted in A.T. Robertson, *Studies in the Epistle of James*, p. 140.

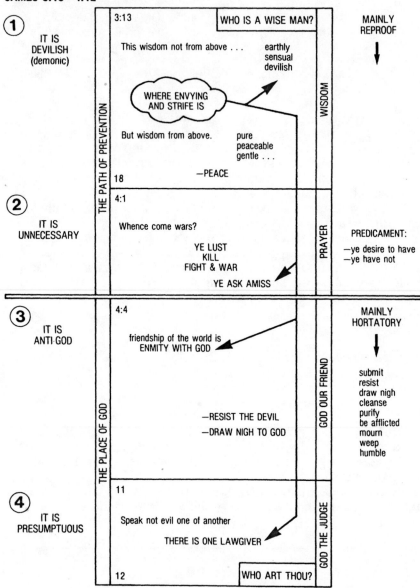

① IT IS DEVILISH (demonic)

3:13 WHO IS A WISE MAN?

This wisdom not from above . . . earthly sensual devilish

WHERE ENVYING AND STRIFE IS

But wisdom from above. pure peaceable gentle . . .

18 —PEACE

THE PATH OF PREVENTION

WISDOM

MAINLY REPROOF

② IT IS UNNECESSARY

4:1 Whence come wars?

YE LUST
KILL
FIGHT & WAR
YE ASK AMISS

PRAYER

PREDICAMENT:
—ye desire to have
—ye have not

③ IT IS ANTI·GOD

4:4 friendship of the world is ENMITY WITH GOD

—RESIST THE DEVIL
—DRAW NIGH TO GOD

THE PLACE OF GOD

GOD OUR FRIEND

MAINLY HORTATORY

submit
resist
draw nigh
cleanse
purify
be afflicted
mourn
weep
humble

④ IT IS PRESUMPTUOUS

11 Speak not evil one of another
THERE IS ONE LAWGIVER

12 WHO ART THOU?

GOD THE JUDGE

86

4:4-10

_____

4:11-12

_____

3. Do you see any subject common to the four themes?

_____

_____

Look at the main topical study of Chart P. Observe the title: "Four Arguments Against Selfish Faction." How do the paragraph points, related to this title, represent content of each paragraph?
   Four Arguments Against Selfish Faction
   1. It is devilish.
   2. It is unnecessary.
   3. It is anti-God.
   4. It is presumptuous.
4. Which paragraph contains the largest number of commands?

_____

_____

5. Compare the first two paragraphs with the last two. Which are mainly reproof; and which are mainly hortatory (i.e., with exhortations and commands)?
6. Do you see any references to "brethren" in this segment? Is James still writing to and about Christians? Support your answer with specific statements in the text.

_____

_____

7. Observe James's use of questions. What are some of the values of this teaching method?

_____

_____

_____

8. What paragraphs make reference to God? How is He identified in each?

_____

_____

_____

9. Make a list of everything taught in this segment about the broad subject of *strife*.

10. Refer to Chart P again. Observe the outlines in the two vertical columns:

The Path of Prevention
A. wisdom (3:13-18)
B. prayer (4:1-3)

The Place of God
A. God our Friend (4:4-10)
B. God the Judge (4:11-12)

What do these outlines have to do with the subject of strife among Christians?

_____

_____

Keep the outlines in mind as you study the segment paragraph by paragraph.

B. Paragraph Analysis

1. *Paragraph 3:13-18: Envious faction is devilish.*
Note how often the key word "wisdom" (and related words) appear here.

Note also how the main subject of strife is referred to in the paragraph.

(Even the word "peace," by way of contrast, should be included among these references.) What is meant by this "wisdom"?

_____

_____

How is it related in the paragraph to the main subject of strife (faction)?[2] Observe the alternation:
   v. 13—wisdom
   v. 14—envying and strife
   v. 15—this wisdom not from above
   v. 16—envying and strife
   vv. 17-18—the wisdom from above

In view of the context of this paragraph, who is a wise man (James's original question in v. 13)?

_____

_____

2. The word translated "strife" means "faction." The *Berkeley Version* translates the word as "rivalry," meaning, of course, evil rivalry.

88

Read verse 13. The Greek word translated "knowledge" has the connotation of expert skill. In view of this, account for the exhortation of the last half of verse 13 and the reference to envy in verse 14a. In verse 14, how are the two commands "glory not" and "lie not" related to the condition, "If ye have bitter envying and strife [faction] in your hearts"?

_____

_____

Read this verse in various modern versions.
Read verse 15. What three realms are represented by the words earthly, sensual, devilish (lit. "demonic")?

_____

_____

_____

Read verse 16. How is confusion in a *group* of Christians similar to frustration and tension in the heart of an *individual* Christian?

_____

_____

In verses 17-18, what kind of believer is described? Why is "pure" a first?

_____

2. *Paragraph 4:1-3: Greedy faction is unnecessary.*
The opening question introduces the subject of this paragraph. What is the question? Compare this with the last verse of chapter 3.

_____

_____

What is James's answer to his own question (4:1b)?

_____

_____

Verse 2 and 3 expand on the answer of 4:1b. There is a natural parallelism in the first part of verse 2, which appears when the punctuation of the King James Version is changed. Here is how verse 2a reads in the *New American Standard Bible:*

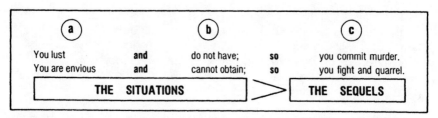

Verses 2*b*-3 follow this with a second parallelism, involving causes:

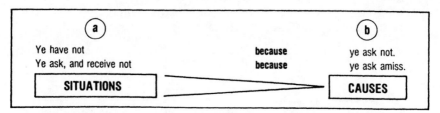

What kind of "wars and fightings" (v. 1) may have been going on among James's readers?

_____

_____

Do you think the phrase "ye kill" (v. 2) has reference to physical murder, or to something else (e.g., hate, 1 John 3:15)?

_____

_____

What is meant by "ye ask amiss" (v. 3)?

_____

_____

How does the last phrase of verse 3 shed light on its meaning?

_____

_____

Think about the logic of James's discourse in 4:1-3:
   a. What you really need, you may have.
   b. You may have what you need by asking for it aright.
   c. Wars and fightings, waged in order to get, are therefore unnecessary.
3. *Paragraph 4:4-10: Proud faction is anti-God.*
James makes no specific reference in this paragraph to faction

among Christians. But there is a structural continuity from paragraph 4:1-3 to paragraph 4:4-10, which tells us that James is writing the latter paragraph to the same group of readers about things vitally related to the specific problem of the first paragraph (fights and quarrels). In the two preceding paragraphs 3:13-18; 4:1-3) the sin was that of not befriending fellow Christians. In this paragraph James accuses some of his readers of not being friends of God. In their pride they have severed their fellowship with God—no wonder then that they have marred their fellowship with other Christians. What various truths are taught in this paragraph about the relationship that should exist between a Christian and God?

_____

_____

In verse 4, what does James mean by "friendship of the world"?

_____

_____

Why is this equated with "enmity with God"? How is adultery a fitting picture of this relationship? (Read Isa. 54:5; Jer. 3:20; Ezek. 16:22; Hos. 9:1.)

_____

_____

The original intent of verse 5 is not clear, for there are various possible translations (consult various versions). For your present study, use the following reading, which divides verse 5 into two sentences.

verse 5a: "Do you think the Scripture speaketh in vain?" (that is, about the sin of worldliness, v. 4).

verse 5b: "The Spirit which He has caused to dwell in us yearns jealously over us" (Weymouth).

How is this statement related to verse 4?

_____

_____

Read verse 6. Here is a bright reference to a work of God. Compare these three ministries:

"The scripture saith" (v. 5a).
"The spirit . . . dwelleth" (v. 5b).
"He [God] giveth" (v. 6a).

How do these three ministries help the Christian stand against the

91

lures of worldliness? What is the condition for receiving the gracious help of God? (See v. 6b; cf. Prov. 3:34; 1 Pet. 5:5).

If verse 5b should be read as a reference to the evil lust in a man's spirit, how does verse 6 teach God's solution to such a problem?

Verses 7-10 provide a list of many short commands. Study them carefully, and apply them to your life.
a. Compare the first word "submit" (v. 7) with the last word, "up" (v. 10).
b. How can a Christian resist the devil (v. 7)? Read Luke 4:1-13. Will the devil "flee from you" permanently in this life? (Cf. Lk. 4:13).

---

c. What does it mean to "draw nigh to God" (v. 8)?

Are there conditions for maintaining this nearness to God?

---

d. Compare "hands" and "hearts" (v. 8). What does each represent?

---

e. What attitude of heart is commanded in verse 9?

Why is joy not a part of this experience of a Christian?

_____

_f._ Compare "heaviness" (v. 9) with "lift you up" (v. 10). Read Philippians 2:5-11 for a description of the two states of Jesus: humiliation and exaltation.
4. *Paragraph 4:11-12: Accusatory faction is presumptuous.*
What are the repeated words of this paragraph?

_____

_____

What is the "law" here?

_____

Who is the "one lawgiver"?

_____

Who alone is the judge of a transgression of God's law?

_____

When a Christian accuses or criticizes a fellow believer, what is he presuming?

_____

_____

What three offices of God are represented by these three terms: lawgiver, save, destroy (v. 12)?

_____

_____

How is the question, "Who art thou?" (v. 12) a soul-searching conclusion to James's treatise on factions among his Christian readers? Relate this question to the opening question of the segment, "Who is a wise man?" (3:13).

III. NOTES

1. "Strife" (3:14). A more accurate translation would be "faction" or "rivalry." Vincent points out that the Greek word in its first-century usage applied to those who "serve in official positions for their own selfish interest, and who, to that end, promote

93

party spirit and faction."[3] Verse 14 reads thus in the *Berkeley Version:* "But if you cherish bitter jealousy and rivalry in your hearts, do not pride yourselves in this and play false to the truth."

2. "Lusteth to envy" (4:5). If this is a reference to evil desire, then the "spirit" is man's spirit.[4] If the "Spirit" is the Holy Spirit, then the phrase translated "lusteth to envy" cannot have an evil intention. See 2 Corinthians 11:2 for a reference to "godly jealousy." On the James passage, Andrew McNab writes:

> In this case the reference is to the gracious work of the Holy Spirit who is grieved and distressed when we prove unfaithful to Christ and to God who has blessed us so richly. He years over us with a holy envy or jealousy to have us wholly for Himself, for He cannot be satisfied with a divided loyalty.[5]

3. "Be afflicted, and mourn" (4:9). This is a call to repentance, an attitude of change of heart referred to in the preceding verses. "The memory of former compromise with the world emphasized the need for deep and true repentance. . . . The true penitent does not venture so much as to lift up his eyes to heaven. There is nothing uplifted about him until God's pardon and grace raise him to his feet."[6]

IV. FURTHER ADVANCED STUDY

The following words appearing in this passage are recommended for word study: truth, evil, peace, envy, humble, pure, judge.

Two important doctrines which may be studied are:

1. The indwelling ministry of the Holy Spirit (e.g., see John 7:39; 16:7; Rom. 8:11; 1 Cor. 3:16; Gal. 4:6; Eph. 3:17; 4:30).

2. Repentance. This subject may be studied under three headings. (Verses shown are a partial list of references.)

Change of view (the intellectual element: Rom. 3:20; Ps. 51:3, 7; Job 42:5-6; Luke 15:17-18).

Change of feeling (the emotional element: Ps. 51:1-2; 2 Cor. 7:9-10; Matt. 21:30, 32; 27:3; 2 Cor. 7:8; Heb. 7:21).

Change of will (the volitional element: Matt. 3:8, 11; Acts 5:31; 20:21; Rom. 2:4; 2 Cor. 7:9-10; 2 Pet. 3:9; Matt. 3:2; Luke 13:2; 15:7; Acts 2:38; 17:30; Rev. 2:5).

3. Marvin R. Vincent, *Word Studies in the New Testament*, 1: 754.
4. See the translation in *Today's English Version.*
5. Andrew McNab, "The General Epistle of James" in *The New Bible Commentary*, p. 1125.
6. Ibid.

Other verses to study in connection with repentance are: Matthew 12:41; Luke 24:47; Acts 2:37; 2 Timothy 2:25; Hebrews 12:10-11.

V. APPLICATIONS

We are well aware that prevention of an evil situation is far more desirable than a cure. James's words are mainly those of cure because the disease of faction has already set in. Nevertheless, James teaches much that can be used a *prevention* of evil. Read the passage again, and list all the truths that when applied to the lives of Christians, would prevent antagonisms in the Christian fellowship.

VI. WORDS TO PONDER

The reason you don't have what you want is because you don't ask God for it. And when you do ask you don't get it because your whole aim is wrong—you want only what will give you pleasure (James 4:2b-3, *Living Bible*).

Lesson 9

James 4:13–5:12

Faith and the Future

This passage is a fitting climax to the epistle since it projects present living into the all-important future. We have seen over and over again that the main burden of the epistle concerns Christian living *today—now*—in the *present*. In fact, the concluding segment of the epistle, 5:13-20, returns to that theme by giving additional specific appeals for Christ-honoring *deeds*. So the passage of this lesson, on the subject of the future, is a peak in the progress of James's letter.

It is not surprising that this much of the last of James's epistle is devoted to teachings about the future. For James wants his readers to have the total picture, involving past, present, and future. They knew the past, which included Christ's redeeming work and their personal experience of regeneration. He has been writing up to this point in the epistle about their present living. So now is the opportune time for him to show his readers how their *todays* are related to their *tomorrows* and to the all-important *Big Tomorrow*, ushered in by the return of the Lord.

Observe that James devotes comparatively little space here to the historical facts of Jesus' atoning work, not because these are unimportant or even irrelevant, but because the divine purpose of his particular book in the New Testament canon is to emphasize the rightful place of *works* in *everyday living*. It is simply a matter of *emphasis* by *quantity*. God could have inspired James to write a long epistle, devoting much space to history and doctrine, but He did not do so.

I. PREPARATION FOR STUDY

1. Review survey Chart G, to orient your thinking in terms of the epistle as a whole. Chart Q is an excerpt from the survey chart.

96

1:1	1:19	4:13	5:13 5:20
PRINCIPLES INVOLVED	PRACTICES FOR THE PRESENT	PRIZES IN THE FUTURE	A CONSTRUCTIVE CONCLUSION
motives for works	the place of works	judgments of works	outreach of works

2. Spend some time thinking about the subject of the "future." Is the future a fact? Is tomorrow as real as yesterday or today? Literally, in terms of clock measurement, what is the closest *future moment* to the split second in which you read the end of this sentence?
What is time?

_____

_____

What is eternity?

_____

_____

What is God's relation to time and eternity?

_____

_____

What is the meaning of God's words "I AM THAT I AM" (Ex. 3:14)?

_____

_____

Why is a person's surety about the future dependent on his relation to God?

_____

_____

II. ANALYSIS

Segment to be analyzed: 4:13–5:12
Paragraph divisions: at verses 4:13; 5:1, 7

97

A. General Analysis

1. Use a work sheet of some sort to record your studies of this passage. (Chart R is a partially completed analytical chart of this segment.)

2. Read the segment for general impressions. Record the main theme of each paragraph:

4:13-17

_____

5:1-6

_____

5:7-12

_____

Note that verse 12 is included in the last paragraph. Often it is printed alone in the Bible text. Do you see any connection between the subject of swearing (v. 12) and the exhortation to be patient (vv. 7-11)? (See Notes for more on this.)

_____

3. Determine from the text whether believers or unbelievers are addressed in each paragraph. Justify your answers. What particular group is the subject of 5:1-6?

_____

4. What references to the future are made in each paragraph?

_____

_____

How are the second and third paragraphs alike in this respect?

_____

How is the first paragraph different from these?

_____

5. The first paragraph talks about the _unknown_ future ("ye know not what," 4:14). How does this differ from the other two paragraphs?

_____

_____

98

6. Compare "miseries" (second paragraph) and "precious fruit" (third paragraph).

_____

_____

7. What is the atmosphere of each paragraph?

_____

_____

B. Paragraph Analysis

Refer to Chart R and observe the main topical study with the title "What About the Future?" What are the paragraph points under this title?

_____

_____

1. *Paragraph 4:13-17*
What tone or attitude is implied in the statement beginning with "To day" (v. 13)? Let verses 16 and 17 help you in answering this question.

_____

_____

Compare the phrases "we will" (v. 13) and "if the Lord will" (v. 15). the key intervening phrase is "ye know not what" (v. 14). What point is James making here?

_____

_____

Is he speaking against making plans per se?

_____

_____

James asks a very important question in verse 14. What natural phenomena common to everyday living are suggested by the illustration of vapor? What is the main point of James's answer? What lessons can a Christian learn from that answer?

_____

_____

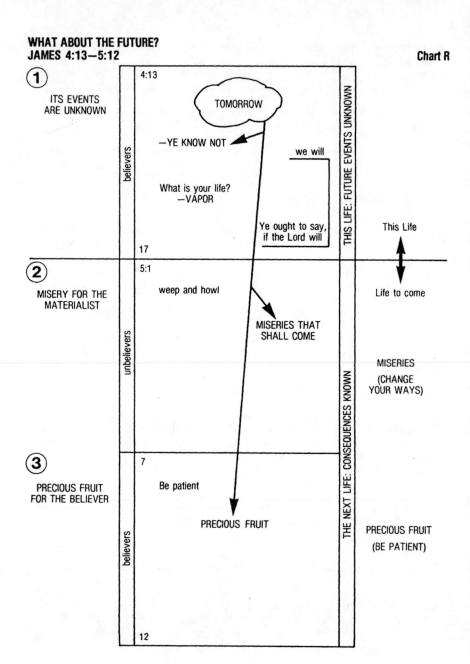

① ITS EVENTS ARE UNKNOWN

② MISERY FOR THE MATERIALIST

③ PRECIOUS FRUIT FOR THE BELIEVER

4:13

believers

TOMORROW

—YE KNOW NOT

we will

What is your life?
—VAPOR

Ye ought to say,
if the Lord will

17

5:1

weep and howl

unbelievers

MISERIES THAT
SHALL COME

7

Be patient

believers

PRECIOUS FRUIT

12

THIS LIFE: FUTURE EVENTS UNKNOWN

THE NEXT LIFE: CONSEQUENCES KNOWN

This Life

Life to come

MISERIES

(CHANGE
YOUR WAYS)

PRECIOUS FRUIT

(BE PATIENT)

What attitude of heart is James appealing to in verse 15?

_____

_____

Is the making of plans excluded from such an attitude?

_____

_____

2. *Paragraph 5:1-6*
Compare the opening of this paragraph with that of the first. Analyze this paragraph with time references in mind. Record your observations below. An example is cited.

Past and Present	Future
weep and howl	miseries shall come upon you
wealth decayed garments moth eaten stolen by greedy merriment and luxury	stored up treasure for last days Lord hears the cries murdered the righteous one

What is the basic sin described in this paragraph?

_____

_____

What main truth is James teaching here?

_____

_____

_____

3. *Paragraph 5:7-12*
How does the tone of this paragraph compare with the previous one?

_____

_____

What is the opening command?

_____

_____

How is the subject of patience developed throughout the paragraph? Record your observations:

v. 7 _____

v. 8 _____

v. 9 _____

v. 10 _____

v. 11 _____

v. 12 _____

What is meant by the phrase "the coming of the Lord"?

_____

_____

Why the commands "be patient" and "stablish your hearts"?

_____

_____

What do verses 10 and 11 suggest as to what some of James's readers were experiencing at this time?

_____

_____

How can happiness (v. 11) co-exist with affliction (v. 10)?

_____

_____

Is any sign of impatience suggested by the act of swearing (v. 12)?

_____

_____

Compare verse 12 with verse 9.

III. NOTES

1. "Buy and sell" (4:13). The illustration in this verse is that of the itinerant Jewish merchants who traveled from city to city in connection with their trade.

2. "The early and latter rain" (5:7). The farmer of Palestine depended on two seasons of rain: the early fall rain, which came after his crops were planted; and the latter spring rain, which came when the crops were maturing. One can see where much patience was needed over this extended period of time before the "precious fruit" was harvested.

3. "Swear not" (5:12). *The New Bible Commentary* sees this verse as related to the context of the subject of patience:

> In excitement and irritation (cf. verse 9) there was always the temptation to lose control of the tongue, a sin against which James has already clearly written. Hence the practical exhortation of verse 12. They were to be content with simplicity of truthful utterance and were to refrain from making any oath either in the name of heaven or of earth.[1]

IV. FURTHER ADVANCED STUDY

A subject recommended for study is the second coming of the Lord, especially with reference to judgment of the unbeliever and rewards for the believer. Among the New Testament books to be consulted are 1 and 2 Thessalonians and 2 Peter.

V. APPLICATIONS

1. What do you think is a healthy attitude for a Christian to have with respect to business ventures and material gains?

2. In what ways should God be a part of our plans, whether they be small or big?

3. Does the attitude behind the words "If the Lord will" discourage activity, planning, and working?

4. Patience is a golden virtue. How can one attain and develop this? Read what Paul writes about patience in Romans 5:3-5.

5. How do the following phrases describe much of society today: "Ye have heaped treasure" (5:3); "Ye have lived in pleasure" (5:5)? What is the message of the gospel to the tragic situation of 5:1-6?

1. Abraham McNab, "The General Epistle of James," in *The New Bible Commentary*, p. 1127.

VI. WORDS TO PONDER

Keep your hopes high, for the day of the Lord's coming is near (5:8, *Today's English Version*).

Lesson 10

Christians Helping Each Other

As James concludes his epistle he is tenderly moved as he reflects on his brethren's physical-spiritual needs. But, in true optimist fashion, he does not linger very long over the problems. To James, problems are the challenges for solutions. And solutions are the demonstrations of a faith that saves. So he devotes these last lines of the epistle to exhort his Christian brethren to help each other in their pressing needs by applying basic principles of the gospel of Christ.

Another observation may be made here concerning James's choice of the subject with which to close his epistle. The particular subject of 5:13-18 is that of *prayer*, a ministry so vital to James that he may have thus wanted to let it be the last note of his appeal. (Recall the tradition that James's knees were worn hard as a camel's from kneeling in prayer for long periods of time.)

I. PREPARATION FOR STUDY

1. Recall from the last lesson that the passage 4:13–5:12 was a peak or climax of the epistle, teaching truths about the *future*, such as the second coming of the Lord Jesus. Return to a discussion about practical everyday affairs, which is the subject of our present passage, could then be called an anticlimax, not any less important than the climax of 4:13–5:12.

2. Read 1 Kings 17 and 18 as background for the illustration of Elijah that James uses in verses 17 and 18.

II. ANALYSIS

Segment to be analyzed: 5:13-20
Paragraph divisions: at verses 13, 19

A. General Analysis

Read the segment first for main impressions and overall purposes.
Observe all the references to the fellowship of believers.
Think back over this passage (5:13-20) and the verses preceding it (5:7-12). Write what you have learned here about:

> Faith
> Hope
> Love

B. Paragraph Analysis

1. *Paragraph 5:13-18*
What is the key repeated word of this paragraph?

_____

Compare the three situations of verses 13-14. Record these:

Is any _____? let him _____.

Is any _____? let him _____.

Is any _____? let him _____;

let them _____.

Observe the combination of supplication (v. 13*a*) and praise (v. 13*b*).
Why is praise such an important ingredient of prayer?

_____

_____

Observe the four references to these subjects (person or group) in verse 14: individual believers ("any among you"); elders; church; Lord. How does verse 14 illustrate the way a local church can minister to its members?

_____

_____

Is anointing oil a magical or supernatural ingredient of the healing process in verses 14-15? If not, what is the purpose of the oil?

_____

_____

Compare Mark 6:13. Then read Isaiah 1:6 and Luke 10:34. How do the last two passages refer to a different situation than that of the James and Mark verses?

_____

List all the conditions for answered prayer that are stated or implied in verses 13-18.

_____

_____

_____

In verse 14, who initiates the prayer session? Who prays? Do you think the sick one prays also? What is meant by the phrase "in the name of the Lord"?

_____

_____

Why does James relate it to the anointing ministry?

_____

_____

Read verse 15a. Contemplate the weighty phrase "the prayer of faith." Who must have faith—the sick person, the elders, or both? Try to think of examples of healing in the ministry of Jesus for help in answering this. In all cases, who is the healer?

_____

_____

See the second part of verse 15. Why does James bring the subject of sins into his discussion of healing? (Read Luke 5:18-26 in this connection.)

_____

_____

Is a repentant spirit of confession of sins a condition for God's forgiving?

_____

_____

Is such a spirit implied in "the prayer of faith"?

_____

_____

What condition in the fellowship of believers does James cite in verse 16a for effective intercessory prayer? (Note: The word translated "faults" is better translated "sins," as in Eph. 1:7; 2:5; Col.

2:13.) What kinds of sins do you think should be confessed to fellow believers; to what extent; and how?

In the translation of verse 16*b*, most versions bring out the intention of the original Greek. Here are two such renderings:

"The supplication of a righteous man availeth much in its working" (ASV*).

"An upright man's prayer, when it keeps at work, is very powerful" (Williams).

What truths about prayer are emphasized here?

What is the point of the phrase "when it keeps at work"?[1]

Read verses 17-18. What is James's purpose in saying that Elijah (Elias) "was a man subject to like passions as we are"?

What truths about prayer are illustrated in this story of Elijah?

How is the story an illustration of verse 16*b*?

2. *Paragraph 5:19-20*

Observe the two verbs of verse 19. Note how these read in the *Berkeley Version:* "My brothers, if one of you strays from the truth and someone brings him back." According to verse 19, who are the ones who had strayed from the truth: Christians or non-

---

*American Standard Version.
1. This phrase is translated ambiguously in the AV as "effectual."

Christians? If Christians, what was their spiritual condition, and how would you describe their relationship to Christ?

What two deliverances of grace come to the restored backslider?

What is meant by "save a soul from death" in this context?

On the phrase "hide a multitude of sins," compare Psalm 32:1; 85:2; Proverbs 10:12, where the word "cover" is used. What spiritual qualities would motivate a Christian to respond to James's appeal to help backsliders?

Compare the situations described in verses 13-14 (trouble) and verses 19-20 (apostasy). Which is the worse condition? Which is more difficult to correct, and why?

III. NOTES

1. "Afflicted" (5:13). The word means "suffering hardship." (Cf. 2 Tim. 2:9; 4:5).

2. "Elders of the church" (5:14). This phrase reveals that the local church was an organized institution as early as the writing of the epistle (A.D. 45-50).

3. "Anointing him with oil" (5:14). The good Samaritan applied oil to the wounded traveler for medicinal purposes (Luke 10:34). James's primary reference to oil is in its symbolic significance, oil being identified with healing.

4. "And if he have committed sins" (5:15). The person's sickness may have been occasioned by an act of sin, but not necessarily so (cf. John 9:1-3). In any case, if the person was spiritually sick

(in a state of having committed sins) as well as physically sick, he could be restored wholly—soul and body.

5. "Elias . . . prayed earnestly" (5:17). The story of Elijah in 1 Kings 17-18 records miracles both of drought and rain, but no specific reference is made to Elijah's praying for these.[2] The James reference is not contradictory. Whatever was James's source of information, the intercessions were factual, or they would not be so recorded in the divinely inspired book.

6. "Shall save a soul from death" (5:20). Three different interpretations of this phrase are cited here:

a. The soul of a backsliding Christian may be delivered from the "realm of death," that is, spiritual death.[3]

b. The soul of an unsaved sinner may be saved from eternal death.[4]

c. A believer may be delivered from premature physical death. On this view *The Wycliffe Bible Commentary* says, "Since the NT teaches the security of the believer in Christ, it is best to take the reference to death as physical death. The early church believed and taught that persistence in sin could cause premature physical death (cf. 1 Cor. 11:30)."[5]

IV. FURTHER ADVANCED STUDY

Three important subjects for study suggested by this passage are: prevailing prayer, divine healing, and apostasy (or backsliding). The responsibility of Christians toward backslidden brethren is taught in such verses as Matthew 18:15-18; 1 Thessalonians 5:14; 2 Thessalonians 3:13-16; Hebrews 10:24.

V. APPLICATIONS

1. What are you obligations to Christians of your acquaintance and local fellowship?

2. Do you find it easy to help and pray for Christians who have strayed from the truth?

3. Do you believe that God can still perform instantaneous miracles of physical healing today? Why are these not as common as in the days of Jesus and the apostles?

2. Henry Alford says that prayer for rain may perhaps only be implied in 1 Kings 38:42 *(The Greek Testament*, 4: 329).
3. Alexander Ross, *The Epistles of James and John*, p. 103.
4. See footnote on James 5:20, *The Westminster Study Edition of the Holy Bible* (Philadelphia: Westminister Press, 1948).
5. Walter W. Wessel, "The Epistle of James," in *The Wycliffe Bible Commentary*, p. 1439.

4. Write a list of conditions for prevailing prayer.

5. What is faith, and why is it the foundation of Christian living?

VI. A FINAL THOUGHT

We have come to the end of James's letter. The very last word of that letter is "sins," a word that represents the main reason for the letter in the first place. The varieties of conditions and circumstances written about in the epistle are legion, moving from *persecution* in 1 1, where the Christians are identified as being scattered around the world, to *apostasy* in 5:19-20, where some among that group are seen as drifting away from the Christian fellowship.

James coveted for his readers nothing but God's best. He wanted to see them growing spiritually, well rounded and balanced, lacking nothing. His warnings and exhortations were serious, frank, and sometimes sharp, but always from the heart of a brother in Christ yearning for the peace and happiness of his brethren.

There is no statistic to tell us the effect of James's letter in the lives of his Jewish friends to whom he wrote. Nor is there a statistic to measure the full impact of the epistle on the church for nearly two millennia. In both cases the fruit is glorious and eternal. But the *issue of the moment* is more personal and can be stated in a simple question:

Has my study of James made *me* a better Christian?

If it has, *it will show* because, in the words of James, "Faith without works is dead."

Bibliography

COMMENTARIES AND TOPICAL STUDIES

Hiebert, David E. *The Epistle of James: Tests of a Living Faith*. Chicago: Moody, 1979.

Luck, G. Coleman. *James: Faith in Action*. Everyman's Bible Commentary. Chicago: Moody, 1969.

McNab, Andrew. "The General Epistle of James." In *The New Bible Commentary*, edited by F. Davidson. Grand Rapids: Eerdmans, 1953.

Moo, Douglas J. *Letter to James*. Grand Rapids: Eerdmans, 1987.

Robertson, A.T. *Studies in the Epistle of James*. Nashville: Broadman, 1959.

Ross, Alexander. "The Epistle of James and John." In *The New International Commentary on the New Testament*. Grand Rapids: Eerdmans, 1954.

Tasker, R.V.G. *The General Epistle of James*. Tyndale New Testament Commentaries. Grand Rapids: Eerdmans, 1956.

Wessel, Walter W. "The Epistle of James." In *The Wycliffe Bible Commentary*, edited by C. F. Pfeiffer and E. F. Harrison. Chicago: Moody, 1962.

RESOURCES FOR FURTHER STUDY

Everyday Bible. New Testament Study Edition. Minneapolis: World Wide, 1988.

Irving L. Jensen, *General Epistles*. Do-It-Yourself Bible Studies. San Bernardino: Here's Life, 1985.

Jensen's Survey of the New Testament. Chicago: Moody, 1981.

New International Version Study Bible. Grand Rapids: Zondervan, 1985. *Ryrie Study Bible*. Chicago: Moody, 1985.

Strong, James. *The Exhaustive Concordance of the Bible*. New York: Abingdon, 1890.

Thiessen, Henry C. *Introductory Lectures in Systematic Theology*. Grand Rapids: Eerdmans, 1956.

Unger, Merrill F. *New Unger's Bible Dictionary*. Chicago: Moody, 1988.

Vincent, Marvin R. *Word Studies in the New Testament*. Grand Rapids: Eerdmans, 1946.

Vine, W.E. *An Expository Dictionary of New Testament Words*. Westwood: N.J.: Revell, 1940.

Printed in the United States
148736LV00002B/3/A